SIMPLY WONDERFUL RECIPES

FOR

WONDERFULLY SIMPLE FOODS

By

Robert Quarry

PREFACE

I realize most people never read prefaces to books, but I hope you will give just a few seconds to reading this one.

Not that you will find deathless prose in the next few paragraphs. It is only that I feel compelled to explain my reasoning in putting this cookbook together.

You will not find anything resembling "Haute Cuisine", "Nouvelle Cuisine" or any other "Cuisine of the moment" recipes in this little book. A stew will be called a stew, not a "Ragout". A pork roast will not masquerade as "Roti du Porc", nor will eggs be referred to as "Oeufs".

There will be no mention of Quiche. Sushi or Thai recipes requiring Lemon Grass.

I had originally planned to title this book "The Little Bit of Difference Cookbook" because it seemed to say exactly what the content (and intent) would be.

The recipes presented here will, I hope, not be too mind-boggling. They do have different degrees of difficulty; but I think I have laid them out in clear and easy steps. They are, basically, recipes for foods we all know, but ones that, with a few adjustments, take on a more intriguing "attitude".

So much for the Preface.

Bon Appetit (OOPS!)...I mean eat and enjoy!

Robert Quarry
Los Angeles — 1988

BREAKFASTS AND BRUNCHES

Nutritionists will tell you breakfast is the most important meal of the day, yet most people will respond to that statement with "Who's got the time?"

I realize many of you have been deluded into thinking that a glass of juice, a cup of coffee and a doughnut is the quick answer. It's quick, all right, but that is the most you can say for it!

Really good muffins, for instance, can be baked ahead of time, frozen and reheated later. Suddenly, with a little planning ahead, the thought of making a pancake or a waffle or a tasty biscuit seems to be a bit less time-consuming.

Of course you can find all of these things in the frozen food section at your grocery markets, but the muffins are distinguishable only by the little bits of things thrown in them, and the only difference between the pancakes and the waffles is their shape.

Cereals do seem to be the expedient thing for a child's breakfast (or your own), but surely you've noticed the rising costs of those T.V. hyped products. I suggest you buy the simple, plain cereals and add your own raisins, nuts, fruits, honey, brown sugar. etc., and save a third off the price of the packaged cereal.

My grandmother used to make a simple but tasty combination to add to any hot cereal. She would take 4 or 5 unpeeled apples, core them, chop them, saute them lightly in a little butter until the bits of apple were barely softened, sprinkle with a little sugar and cinnamon, and then store the mixture in a covered container in the "ice-box".

With the addition of a heaping tablespoon of this heavenly stuff to any cooked cereal, the dreaded "mush" became a looked-forward-to treat.

So much for the practical side of breakfast! Let' s proceed to the real "goodies".

These bran muffins require a bit more time, but they are worth the effort. And remember, they can be frozen.

HONEY-GLAZED BRAN MUFFINS

INGREDIENTS:

> 1 cup all-bran
> 1 cup buttermilk
> 1 cup all-purpose flour
> 1 tsp. cinnamon
> 1 tsp. baking powder
> ½ tsp. baking soda
> ½ tsp. salt
> ⅓ cup butter, room temperature
> ½ cup brown sugar
> 1 large egg
> ¼ cup molasses
> ⅓ cup raisins
> ⅓ cup chopped dates

GLAZE:

> ¼ cup honey
> ⅓ cup corn syrup (dark preferred)
> 1 Tbsp. butter

PREPARATION:

Step 1: Preheat oven to 400°. Line muffin pan with 12 paper baking cups.

Step 2: Combine bran and buttermilk.

Step 3: Mix together flour, cinnamon, baking powder, baking soda and salt. Add all at once to bran mixture, stirring just to mix.

Step 4: Cream butter, brown sugar, egg and molasses thoroughly. Blend into bran mixture. Stir in raisins and dates.

Step 5: Fill muffin cups ¾ full. Bake 20 to 25 minutes. Cool slightly. Remove papers. Muffins can be frozen at this point.

Step 6: If muffins are to be used immediately glaze with following.

GLAZE: In small saucepan combine honey, corn syrup and butter. Bring to boil over medium heat. Reduce heat and simmer 5 minutes. Place muffin tops one at a time in glaze, using a spoon to coat each one thoroughly. Place on cookie sheet until glaze is set. Serve warm with butter.

CHEESE-FILLED BACON MUFFINS

INGREDIENTS:

                3 cups pancake mix
                1 cup milk
                ⅔ cup bacon drippings
                2 eggs
                1 pound bacon, cooked, drained and crumbled
                ⅓ cup finely chopped green pepper
                ⅓ cup finely chopped onion
                2 ounces Cheddar cheese, cut into 18 cubes.

PREPARATION:

Step 1: Fry bacon until crisp. Drain on paper toweling, and crumble. Reserve ⅔ cup drippings.

Step 2: Combine pancake mix, milk, bacon drippings and eggs in large bowl. Stir just until blended.

Step 3: Add bacon, green pepper and onion and stir to blend.

Step 4: Spoon batter into 6 greased 4¼-inch baking cups, filling ⅔ full. Press 3 cheese cubes into each muffin.

Step 5: Place on jellyroll pan and bake at 400° 25 minutes or until golden brown. Remove from pans immediately. Makes 6 muffins.

As you can probably imagine these muffins are a meal in themselves!

BLUEBERRY MUFFINS

INGREDIENTS:

                1 cup granulated sugar
                1 cup vegetable shortening
                1 tsp. salt
                3 whole eggs.
                1 cup milk
                4 cups **cake flour**
                1 Tbsp. baking powder
                1 pound frozen or fresh blueberries

PREPARATION:

Step 1: Cream sugar with shortening and salt. Gradually add eggs, one at a time, mixing well. Scrape sides of bowl to mix well.

Step 2: Combine flour and baking powder. Add milk slowly to flour mixture and blend well, alternating with sugar-shortening mixture.

Step 3: Fold blueberries carefully into batter.

Step 4: Divide mixture into well-greased or paper-lined muffin tins and bake at 400° 25 to 30 mins. Makes about 22 muffins.

These muffins freeze beautifully. Serve them warm.

These muffins were served at the famous Biltmore Hotel in Los Angeles and they truly are better than Sara's.

Now let's proceed to other things...pancakes and waffles.

GINGERBREAD PANCAKES

INGREDIENTS:

> 1 cup whole-wheat flour
> ¾ tsp. baking soda
> ½ tsp. ground ginger
> ½ tsp ground cinnamon
> ¼ tsp. ground cloves
> ¼ tsp. salt
> 2 tsp. instant coffee granules
> ¼ cup hot water
> 1 (6-ounce can) frozen unsweetened apple juice concentrate, thawed
> 2 Tbsps. margarine, melted.

PREPARATION:

Step 1: Combine flour, baking soda, ginger, cinnamon, cloves and salt in large mixing bowl.

Step 2: In a smaller bowl dissolve instant coffee in the hot water. Add egg, thawed apple juice concentrate and melted margarine, and mix well.

Step 3: Add liquid ingredients to dry ingredients and mix just enough to moisten. Mixture will be lumpy.(If batter is too thick, thin with **small amount** of water.)

Step 4: Pour batter, ¼ cup at a time, onto hot skillet or griddle that has been sprayed with non-stick vegetable coating. Cook until the top of each pancake is covered with tiny bubbles and the bottom is brown. Turn and brown the other side. Pancakes ,will be soft, so use a wide enough spatula.

Serve with apple butter and very soft whipped cream cheese.

BAKED PANCAKE

INGREDIENTS:

2 Tbsps. vegetable oil
2 eggs
1 cup milk
½ cup flour
½ cup of flaked whole grain cereal, crushed

PREPARATION:

Step 1: Place 1 Tbsp.of oil in 9 inch glass baking dish. Heat in 425° oven while preparing batter.

Step 2: Place eggs in fairly small bowl and beat with electric beater set at medium speed for 30 seconds. Continue beating while adding milk and remaining 1 Tbsp. oil.

Step 3: Gradually add flour and cereal, mixing until combined.

Step 4: Remove hot baking dish from oven. Pour in batter. Return to oven and bake 25 to 30 mins. or until golden brown. Serve with any fruited yogurt of your choice.

BREAKFAST PANCAKE
(2 servings)

INGREDIENTS:

½ cup all purpose flour
½ cup milk
2 eggs lightly beaten
Pinch of grated nutmeg.
½ stick of butter (2 oz.)
2 Tbsps. powdered sugar.
Juice of half a lemon.
Marmalade (garnish)

PREPARATION:

Step 1: Preheat oven to 425°

Step 2: Combine flour, milk, eggs and nutmeg in medium bowl and beat lightly(batter will be lumpy).

Step 3: Melt butter in oven proof skillet (12 inch. skillet) over medium-high heat.

Step 4: Pour batter into hot skillet. Place in oven and bake pancake until golden brown,about 15 to 20 mins.

Step 5: Sprinkle sugar evenly over top of pancake and continue baking until sugar melts, about one minute.

Step 6: Squeeze lemon juice over top and serve immediately with marmalade on the side.

THE BEST FRENCH TOAST, EVER

INGREDIENTS:

> 8 slices of French bread (one inch thick),
> preferably a day or more old, crusts removed
> 4 eggs, beaten lightly
> 1 cup half and half.
> ¼ tsp. salt
> a pinch of cardamom
> ½ tsp vanilla
> Butter or margarine.

PREPARATION:

Step 1: Preheat oven to 400°

Step 2: Combine eggs, half and half, cardamom, and vanilla

Step 3: Dip bread slices in mixture. Place slices in glass baking dish large enough to accommodate the bread in a single layer, and pour remaining liquid over pieces. Let bread absorb all liquid.

Step 4: Fry in butter over medium heat. When brown on one side, turn and brown second side. (turn only once.)

Step 5: Drain bread on paper towel and place on baking sheet and allow to puff up in 400° oven for 5 mins.

Step 6: Drain again on paper towel to absorb excess fat. Sprinkle with powdered sugar and serve immediately with jelly or syrup.

(Note: If cardamom is unavailable, a pinch of nutmeg may be substituted.)

If you have a fondness for waffles as I do, here are a few recipes that require no more work than the every-day waffle. And as most waffle-irons have non-stick surfaces the cleaning up process is at a minimum.

BANANA WAFFLES

INGREDIENTS:

> 2 cups Biscuit Mix
> 1½ cups buttermilk
> 1 egg
> 1 banana, mashed until smooth
> Spiced bananas

PREPARATION:

Step 1: Combine Bisuit Mix, buttermilk, egg, and banana in large bowl and mix until smooth with rotary beater.

Step 2: Using ½ cup per waffle, bake in preheated waffle iron that has been sprayed with non-stick vegetable coating. Waffles are done when golden brown or waffle iron no longer steams. Serve with Spiced Bananas. Makes 6 waffles.

SPICED BANANAS

INGREDIENTS:

> ½ cup frozen apple juice concentrate (undiluted)
> 3 bananas. sliced crosswise
> ¼ tsp. ground cinnnamon
> ¼ tsp. ground allspice
> ⅛ tsp. ground nutmeg
> Dash ground cloves

PREPARATION:

Step 1: Heat apple juice concentrate in skillet. Add banana slices and cook over medium heat until tender. Sprinkle with spices.

Step 2: Divide bananas and sauce into 6 portions and spoon portion over each waffle.

CORNMEAL WAFFLES

INGREDIENTS:

> 1 cup flour
> ¼ cup sugar
> 2 tsp. baking powder
> 1 tsp. baking soda
> ¾ tsp. salt
> 1½ cups cornmeal (white or yellow)
> 2 eggs
> 1½ cups buttermilk
> ⅓ cup vegetable oil

PREPARATION:

Step 1: Mix all the above ingredients and beat with rotary beater until smooth.

Step 2: Bake until golden brown and there is no steam coming from iron. Serve with good maple syrup.

PUMPKIN WAFFLES

For crisp texture, bake these waffles until they're richly browned.

INGREDIENTS:

> 2¼ cups all-purpose flour
> 4 tsps. baking powder
> 2 tsps. ground cinnamon
> 1 tsp. each ground allspice and ginger
> ¼ cup firmly packed brown sugar
> 1 cup canned pumpkin
> 2 cups milk
> 4 eggs, separated
> ¼ cup melted butter

PREPARATION:

Step 1: Stir together the flour, baking powder, cinnamon, allspice, ginger, salt, and sugar.

Step 2: Combine the pumpkin, milk and egg **yolks**; add the flour mixture and butter; stir to blend.

Step 3: Beat the egg whites until soft peaks form; **fold** into batter to blend.

Step 4: Preheat waffle iron. Pour batter onto grill; cook until waffles are richly browned and crisp (about 5 mins.) Makes about 5 waffles.

I like to serve a nut butter with these. Simply blend ½ cup each softened butter or margarine and finely chopped pecans, and ½ tsp. grated orange rind. Spread over waffles and then add syrup.

Now it is time to turn our attention to the ever- popular and con- troversial EGG!

Everyone knows how simple it is to cook an egg, right? WRONG!

First let's start with some of the basic things we should know about the handling and preparation of the egg. For instance; eggs cold from the refrigerator do not cook with the same lightness as those that are at room temperature. When you know ahead of time that you are going to be using eggs leave them in a cool place the night before.

Of course, the most essential thing to me is to have an egg pan. This pan should be used for **nothing** but eggs. An eight inch pan with sloping sides is recommended for omelets and will accommodate at least 3 fried eggs or six scrambled eggs. **Never** wash this pan with soap and water or scrub with a soap pad. Once the pan is "seasoned" simply rinse out with very hot water and go over the surface with a sponge. Even the non-stick variety of pan should be treated in this manner.

Scrambling eggs (or making an omelet) suffers with the addition of milk or cream, whereas the addition of ½ tablespoon of water (per egg) will lighten the texture and produce the fluffiness desired.

It is better to keep the temperature of the pan at medium heat; if the pan is too hot the eggs take on a bitter taste. Try out the pan at varying degrees of heat until you find exactly the right level.

As for hard-boiled eggs, I have found the best way to cook them is to place the eggs in a pan of **cold** water to cover, bring them to a boil, remove from heat, cover them, let them sit for 13 minutes, put them in cold water for three minutes and then return them to the hot water for ten seconds. This way they seem to peel more easily (don't you love the way some hard boiled eggs refuse to seperate from the skin and shell?)

For poached eggs I recommend the addition of a Tbsp. of plain white vinegar to the poaching water. This seems to keep the egg from floating all over the pan and produces the proper shape.

And now for the Omelet, the bane and downfall of most amateur chefs.

To make a **proper** omelet requires **three** eggs. Less than that number might just as well be scrambled with whatever bits of things you wish to use.

Remember, an omelet should be **filled** with good things; not tossed together with "whatever". Prepare the omelet and then add the filling to the center before folding over and serving.

Here is the basic omelet recipe. It may take a little experimenting, but once you get the hang of it, you'll be amazed how simple the process is.

BASIC OMELET

INGREDIENTS:

       3 eggs (room temperature)
       1½ Tbsps. water
       1 Tbsp. butter (I specify butter because some margarines have a high water content.)

PREPARATION:

Step 1: Place omelet pan over low flame to heat.

Step 2: Lightly whisk eggs with a fork until just blended.

Step 3: Turn up heat under pan to medium. Put butter in pan , and when it foams (do not let it brown) pour eggs in and whisk very quickly with the fork as if to scramble, patting the eggs down gently. This will not take longer than a minute. Eggs will look very soft on top, but remember when the omelet is folded over the cooking process will continue.

Step 4. Turn heat off immediately and add any filling you choose to center of omelet.

Step 5. When the filling is in place take a spatula and fold over one side (one third of the omelet), to cover filling. With the spatula, carefully make sure the rest of the omelet is released from the pan. Now gently roll the omelet on to the dish, so that the other side overlaps the first, seam side down.

Step 6: Spread a little soft butter on top of the omelet to give it a nice sheen and serve immediately.

Suggested fillings:

       All fillings should be cooked ahead of time and kept warm until they are to be put in omelet.

1. Thinly sliced mushrooms sauteed in a little butter with just a dash of cayenne pepper and a few drops of lemon juice.

2. Sauteed thinly sliced onion, thinly sliced green pepper and a little peeled and chopped tomato to which you will add enough light tomato sauce and a pinch of cayenne, a pinch of ground cumin seed and a pinch of salt to taste.

3. Ham that has been cut into small chunks and lightly sautéed in butter with just a pinch of clove and a pinch of brown sugar. Place the ham on the omelet and then sprinkle with Swiss cheese (the cheese will melt when the omelet is folded over).

4. Orange marmalade is spread on the omelet and a Tbsp. of softened cream cheese (or sour cream) is spread over the marmalade.

Be creative! Add any kind of grated cheese, fresh herbs, whatever appeals to you. Salt the omelet at the last when the omelet is served. Adding salt to the eggs while cooking tends to toughen the omelet.

I'm going to give you three of my favorite brunch dishes. These should be served with fresh sliced fruit and the standard bacon, ham or sausage. Toasted English muffins are also a nice accompaniment.

CHEESE BLINTZ CASSEROLE
(Advance Preparation Required)

INGREDIENTS:

4 eggs
1½ pints (3 cups) sour cream
¼ cup orange juice
¼ cup sugar
1 tsp. vanilla
½ stick sweet (unsalted) butter, melted
1½ tsp. finely grated orange peel
12 frozen blintzes (These can be found in the frozen food shelf of most major markets. You will want the plain cheese blintzes.)

PREPARATION:

You will need a glass baking dish that will accommodate the blintzes so that they will fit in one layer. If you cut the recipe in half, adjust the size of the baking dish accordingly.

Step 1: In blender mix 4 eggs, sour cream, orange juice, sugar and vanilla. Stir in grated orange peel.

Step 2: Pour melted butter in bottom of casserole, lay blintzes on top of butter and pour sauce over top.

Step 3: Cover casserole with foil paper and put in refrigerator overnight.

Step 4: Preheat oven to 350° and bake casserole for one hour, uncovered.

AUF LAUF
(and don't ask what it means)

INGREDIENTS:

> ½ cup flour
> 5 ounces milk
> 3 Tbsps. Ricotta cheese
> 3 eggs
> 1 tsp. sugar
> pinch of salt
> Scant ½ stick sweet butter, melted

PREPARATION:

Step 1: Blend flour and milk until smooth. Add beaten eggs, salt and sugar. Blend well.

Step 2: Pour butter into 8.inch square baking pan and add batter.

Step 3: Bake in 450° oven for 15 mins (or until lightly browned and puffy).

Step 4: Serve with any favorite jam and sour cream.

(This recipe serves two people, so if you wish to double the recipe adjust size of baking pan accordingly.)

SWEET SPANISH ONION BAKE

INGREDIENTS:

> 2 cups chopped sweet Spanish onions
> ½ cup diced ham
> ½ cup sliced mushrooms
> ⅓ cup sliced celery
> ⅓ cup chopped green pepper
> 1 Tbsp. butter or margarine
> ¼ cup diced pimiento
> 2 cups **toasted** bread cubes
> 1½ cups shredded Swiss cheese
> 6 eggs
> 2 Tbsps. flour
> 1½ cups half and half
> ¼ tsp. salt
> ⅛ tsp freshly ground black pepper
> Sweet Spanish onion rings.

PREPARATION:

Step 1: Saute onions, ham, mushrooms, celery, green pepper and pimiento in butter until onion is golden.

Step 2: Layer bread cubes, cheese and onion mixture in 12-inch heat-proof dish.
Step 3: Beat eggs, flour, half and half, salt and pepper until well blended but not frothy.
Step 4: Pour over onion mixture in baking dish. Arrange onion rings over top for garnish and bake at 350° 25 to 30 minutes or until set and golden. Makes four to six servings.

To finish up this breakfast and brunch segment let me give you a traditional recipe for one of my favorite treats.

POPOVERS

INGREDIENTS:

> 2 large eggs (room temperature)
> ¾ cup milk
> ¼ cup water
> Scant cup of flour
> Pinch of salt

PREPARATION:
Step 1: Mix eggs, milk, water and salt in blender.
Step 2: With blender at low speed, slowly add flour.
Step 3: Let mixture sit in blender for 20 minutes, blend again for a few seconds.
Step 4: Oven must be preheated to 425°. Muffin tins should be oiled with about ¼ inch of vegetable oil left in them and heated in the hot oven for 5 mins.
Step 5: Fill hot muffin tins about ¾ full of batter and quickly put tins back in oven.
Step 6: Let popovers bake for 12 minutes at this temperature and then drop heat to 375° and bake 15 to 20 minutes longer. They will have popped up and turned a beautiful golden brown color.
Step 7: Remove popovers from tins and blot the bottoms very briefly on paper towels. Serve immediately with butter and marmalade, or slice off tops and fill with soft scrambled eggs, replacing tops.

A friend of mine insisted I put in this **silly** recipe, so as a favor to her, and to any of you who like a giggle, here it is.

ONE EYED TOAST

INGREDIENTS:

>   1 piece of grained bread
>   Softened butter
>   1 egg

PREPARATION:

Step 1: With a cookie cutter cut out center of bread (about the circumference of an egg yolk) and butter both sides of bread.

Step 2: Heat small frying pan over moderate heat. Set bread in pan and break egg into the hole. Cook for a minute or two, and then, with a wide spatula, flip it over and cook the other side for the same length of time.

Please promise not to tell anyone where you got this recipe. At least your kids will like it. (I like it, too!)

And there you have a few suggestions for ways to "pep up" breakfasts and brunches. There's nothing wrong with the mundane "Ham 'N eggs", but I think you will enjoy serving something a little different for a change, and I know your family and guests will appreciate it.

SALADS, SOUPS, AND SANDWICHES

Lunch should be the most relaxing time of a busy day; whether at home or at work, "grabbing a fast bite to eat" is not the answer for the tensions accumulated in the morning or those you are about to face in the afternoon.

Give your body and your mind the rest it needs, It's a minor indulgence we can all well afford, and it does save one from ending up the day with nerves as frazzled as the hair you've tried to pull off your head.

If you can't go out to lunch, a little planning ahead can make a noon time break a thing of joy. A nice soup and a sandwich or a refreshing salad are a perfect accompaniment for an hour with your favorite soap-opera or that book you never seem to have time to read.

It may seem a bit incongruous to be thinking of lunch when you're busy getting a breakfast together but, if you've planned ahead, you can manage to prepare **two** meals at the same time and really give yourself a break when noon-time rolls around.

First let us deal with soups. For the most part they are fairly simple to handle and so much better than the canned variety.

I have a simple all-purpose recipe for any creamed soup that would probably send a dyed-in-the-wool gourmet chef into a fit of despair. . .but, trust me, it is an absolutely fail-proof combination, and I have always received compliments from the most finicky of eaters. Tell no one how simple it is and you can fool anyone with this bit of magic.

Incidentally, these recipes for soups and salads can be used as a first course for a dinner party.

BASIC CREAMED SOUP

INGREDIENTS:

> 4 cups of any kind of vegetable
> 1 or 2 leeks (white part only) sliced thinly (if leeks are unavailable use 4 or 5 shallot buds or 1 small white onion thinly sliced)
> 3 cans **condensed** chicken broth
> 1½ **cans** water
> dash of white pepper
> Any herbs of your choice such as thyme, basil, dill, curry, etc.

PREPARATION:

Step 1: Place all ingredients in 4 quart pot. Bring to a boil, cover and let simmer for ½ hour.

Step 2: Put mixture (½ at a time) in blender and puree until velvety smooth. I recommend using the blender instead of food processor as it seems to make a smoother puree.

Step 3: Let mixture cool for 15 mins. Add 1 to 1½ cups of half and half to puree mixture. If mixture is too thick simply add a bit of water. Salt to taste.

When making cream of asparagus or broccoli or cauliflower, save a few tips of asparagus or tiny bits of broccoli or cauliflower that have been lightly sauteed in sweet butter until crisp tender and add to soup at last minute.

Beside the above mentioned vegetables I recommend zucchini, any kind of yellow squash, and carrots.

BEER AND CHEESE SOUP

INGREDIENTS:

> 2 cups milk
> 2 cups dark beer
> 2 cups sharp Chedder cheese, grated
> ⅓ cup cooked crumbled bacon (or finely chopped baked ham)
> ½ cup flour
> ¼ cup melted butter
> Salt to taste

PREPARATION:

Step 1: Combine milk, beer and cheese in medium saucepan. Stir over medium heat until cheese has melted. Stir in bacon or ham bits.

Step 2: Combine flour and melted butter and form into ball. Add butter mixture to warm milk mixture.

Step 3: Cook over **low** heat, stirring constantly, until butter mixture dissolves and soup is thickened. If soup is too thick add a bit more milk.

EASY CRAB BISQUE

INGREDIENTS:
>1 can condensed green pea soup (11¼ ounces)
>1 cup half and half
>2 cans tomato soup (I recommend Andersons)
>1 6½ ounce can crabmeat
>¼ cup sherry

PREPARATION:

Step 1: Mix pea soup and half and half until smooth. Add tomato soup and stir until blended.

Step 2: Bring soup to a simmer and add sherry. Let simmer for five minutes (Do not boil at high temperature)

Step 3: Add crabmeat. Let sit for 15 or 20 mins. Heat and serve.

Here are a few cold soups that I particularly like. Two of them contain vodka, but simply eliminate it if there is any problem with the use of alcohol.

FIRE AND ICE SOUP

This is really a smooth form of Gazpacho (which I love . . . if only it loved me back).

INGREDIENTS:
>6 medium tomatoes, peeled, seeded and chopped
>1 canned green Ortega chile, minced
>½ cucumber, peeled, seeded and chopped
>1 scallion, chopped finely
>1 Tbsp. red wine vinegar
>½ tsp. dried marjoram
>Juice of ½ lemon
>1 cup sour cream
>1 can condensed chicken broth
>¼ cup vodka
>Salt and pepper to taste
>Dash of Tabasco

PREPARATION:

Put all ingredients except sour cream in blender and blend until smooth. Transfer to medium bowl and stir in sour cream and vodka. Season to taste and chill thoroughly before serving.

COLD AVOCADO SOUP

INGREDIENTS:

      2 avocados
      1 medium sized tomato, peeled and chopped
      Juice of ½ lemon
      1 green onion, cut up
      1 can condensed chicken broth
      1 cup sour cream
      1½ Tbsps. Ortega green chile salsa
      Salt and white pepper to taste
      A few drops of green food coloring

PREPARATION:

    Put all ingredients in blender and puree until satin smooth. Add one jigger of vodka (optional) and chill until very cold.

COLD CUCUMBER SOUP

INGREDIENTS:

      3 Tbsps. butter
      1 large leek (white part only)
      4 cucumbers (peeled)
      2 bay leaves
      6 peppercorns
      3 Tbsps. flour
      2 cans condensed chicken broth
      2 **cans** water
      1 cup half and half
      Juice of ½ lemon
      Dash of Tabasco

PREPARATION:

Step 1: Melt butter in large skillet. Add 3 cucumbers, sliced thinly; and thinly sliced leek. Braise over medium low heat with bay leaves and peppercorns.

Step 2: Add flour and stir. Then add chicken broth and water. Simmer for 30 mins.

Step 3: Put mixture in blender and mix until smooth. Pour through strainer into large bowl.

Step 4: Chill soup, then add half and half, lemon juice and dash of Tabasco.

Step 5: Peel remaining cucumber, slice in half the long way and remove seeds with teaspoon. Slice very thinly and add to soup. Chill for several hours.

    Serve in chilled bowls. Top with a dollop of sour cream and sprinkle with chopped chives or fresh dill.

Here are some recipes for hearty soups that can be served as an entire supper.

SPLIT PEA SOUP WITH SPARERIBS
(Advance Preparation Required)

INGREDIENTS:

> One pound yellow or green split peas
> 3 pounds spareribs
> 8 cups water
> 2 stalks celery, cut in chunks
> 2 carrots, cut in chunks
> 4 leeks (white part only) diced
> 1 tsp. hickory smoked salt
> ¼ tsp. thyme
> 2 bay leaves
> 10 sprigs of parsley
> 10 peppercorns

PREPARATION:

Step 1: Cover split peas with cold water and soak overnight.

Step 2: Combine spareribs and the 8 cups of water in a large kettle. Bring to the boil.

Step 3: Drain peas and add to ribs along with celery, carrots, leeks, smoked salt, thyme and regular salt to taste.

Step 4: Tie bay leaves, parsley and whole peperccorns in a small square of cheesecloth and drop into soup.

Step 5: Cover and simmer three to four hours until soup is consistency of thin porridge. Add hot water from time to time if needed.

Step 6: Remove ribs from soup and strip meat from bones. Return meat to pot. Taste and add more salt or hickory salt if needed.

Step 7: Reheat soup, remove bundle of herbs and ladle soup into hot bowls.

MULLIGATAWNY SOUP

INGREDIENTS:

¾ cup dry chick peas or Garbanzo beans
½ cup olive oil
1 cup chopped onion
1 clove minced garlic
1 tsp. minced ginger root
¼ cup curry powder
2 pounds chicken parts
2 quarts chicken broth
1 cup cooked rice

PREPARATION:

Step 1: Grind chick peas in blender until flourlike.

Step 2: Heat olive oil in 4-quart saucepan. Saute onion 5 mins. Add garlic, then mix in ginger and curry powder. Cook 2 mins., stirring constantly.

Step 3: Blend in chickpea flour, then add chicken and chicken broth. Bring to boil, stirring frequently.

Step 4: Cover loosely and cook over low heat 45 mins. Remove and drain chicken. Remove bones and skin, then dice chicken meat.

Step 5: Puree soup in blender until smooth. Return to saucepan and taste to adjust seasonings. Mix in chicken and rice. Reheat and serve with lemon slices on side. (Soup will be on the thick side. Add additional chicken broth, if thinner consistency is desired.)

And now let's discuss the subject of sandwiches. Everyone knows how to make a sandwich...right? Not necessarily! We know it takes two slices of bread and something jammed in between them, but how can we do this with a little more culinary appeal?

The English have a wonderful way with sandwiches...but Americans prefer something a little sturdier. I personally prefer the English method...very thin sliced bread (crusts removed, of course) spread with good sweet butter, filled with thinly sliced tomato or thin slices of crisp cucumber or chopped watercress in enough cream cheese to bind it together.

The sandwiches are then cut into "fingers" and served with lovely freshly brewed tea (no teabags used here, thank you veddy much!).

The American way is much less dainty, however. We like our fillings to be of sturdier stuff — egg salad, tuna salad, chicken salad, ham salad, a nice slice of roast beef or pastrami on rye bread.

The only trouble with this is that we have forgotten that the word "salad" means exactly that. Just mashing up something and binding it together with mayonnaise does not quite "cut it".

There are so many good ingredients to be used. Chopped celery, a little minced green pepper, pimiento, minced chives or scallions, sweet pickle (or dill) finely chopped, (no pickle relish, please) minced water chestnuts, are a few things that should be added to the chopped egg, tuna, ham, shrimp, etc. to make a more savory filling. Experiment with combinations of ingredients and I think you will be pleased with the results.

I happen to have an unfortunate affinity with peanut butter, but then, no one is perfect. Many years ago a wonderful restaurant named Schraffts specialized in peanut butter and banana sandwiches, and, in Hollywood, C.C. Browns was known for its "Boulevard Special" which consisted of peanut butter, jelly, and a slice of cold ham. I'm also fond of peanut butter combined with Chutney and bacon bits.

I mention these things only to give you an idea of how the mundane sandwich can be experimented with, usually with happy results.

I'm going to give you only one recipe for a sandwich that may make you think twice before sending out for pizza. This combination is very rich but heavenly to taste . . . try it with an ice cold glass of cola or better yet, a glass of cold beer!

STUFFED ROLLS

INGREDIENTS:

    10 soft French finger rolls (or sesame rolls)
    1 pound shredded sharp Cheddar cheese
    2 medium white onions, chopped fine
    1 large clove crushed garlic
    2 small cans Ortega green chiles (chopped)
    1 cup minced ripe olives
    1 cup salad oil
    1 can tomato sauce (8 oz.)
    2 Tbsps. red wine vinegar
    Salt
    Dash cayenne pepper

PREPARATION:

Step 1: Slice rolls laterally a third of the way from top and hollow out(from the thick side) enough bread to make room for the filling.

Step 2: Mix all the rest of the ingredients and then fill the hollowed out portion of roll. Place top back on roll.

Step 3: Wrap each roll individually in wax paper. Put rolls in covered baking dish and bake 1 hour in 300-degree oven.

Now we come to the salad bar . . . salads make a wonderful first course for any dinner party, but remember, the success of the salad is very often dependent on the salad dressing. Please, please, I beg of you to resist those bottles of dressing on your market shelf and learn to make your own. Dressings are not difficult, and with your own "home-made" touch you will be rewarded for the tiny bit of work it takes.

Always use a good olive oil (I recommend Bertolli's), a good vinegar, fresh herbs if you can find them, and always freshly ground pepper.

If you don't already possess a lettuce dryer I recommend you buy one. They are not that expensive, and they do make a difference in the crispness of all salad greens.

First let me give you some recipes for some of my favorite salad dressings and then a few recipes for some of my special salads.

SALAD DRESSINGS

One: Carefully mix 1 egg with 1½ cups salad oil and ¼ cup freshly grated Parmesan cheese. Add 1½ Tbsps. lemon juice, ½ tsps. each of A-1 sauce and Worcestershire sauce, 1 mashed garlic clove. 3 drops of Tabasco, and salt and pepper to taste.

Two: Mix 4 Tbsps. each of Dijon mustard and red wine vinegar. Very slowly whisk in ½ cup of olive oil and add black pepper to taste. This is a classic Vinaigrette dressing, delicious when tossed with mixed greens such as arugula, escarole, endive and watercress.

Three: Blend Together
                           ¾ cup mayonnaise
                           2 Tbsps. orange blossom honey
                           2½ Tbsps. Dijon mustard
                           2 tsps. prepared horseradish
                           ½ tsp. white pepper
                           1 tsp. salt
                           2 Tbsps. minced onion
                           ¾ cup parsley (minced)

Four: BASIC RED WINE DRESSING
I always have this dressing in the "fridge". Empty mayonnaise jars make good containers.
                           5 ounces olive oil
                           1 ounce (2 Tbsps.) red wine vinegar
                           2 ounces dry red wine
                           ½ tsp. dry mustard
                           1 tsp. salt
                           ½ tsp. Worcestershire sauce
                           pinch of basil and pinch of tarragon
                           1 tsp. sugar
                           Garlic, mashed (the number of cloves
                           used depends on how much you like gar-
                           lic...start with one clove and then work
                           your way up.)
                           Freshly ground black pepper to taste
Stir all ingredients together until well blended and store in refridgerator.

Five: THOUSAND ISLAND DRESSING
        This is the most abused salad dressing in the world. Most restaurants throw mayonnaise, catsup and a little pickle relish together and call it either 1000 Island dressing or Russian dressing...it is neither!
        The "Island" part refers to all the tiny bits and pieces of good things blended together. My grandmother's recipe is as follows and was always served as a first course poured over very chilled hearts of lettuce.
INGREDIENTS:
                           1 tsp. chopped sweet pickle
                           1 cup mayonnaise
                           3 Tbsps. chili sauce
                           1 Tbsp. minced green pepper
                           1 tsp. chopped pimiento
                           1½ tsps. chopped chives (or minced
                           green onion)

1 Tbsp. chopped ripe olives
1 hard boiled egg, chopped finely
½ cup whipped cream

PREPARATION:

Mix first 7 ingredients together and then fold in whipped cream. Put in container and chill thoroughly. Double recipe when having company.

Six: CHINESE DRESSING
        INGREDIENTS:

10 toasted blanched almonds
3 cloves garlic
¼ tsp Chinese five-spice powder
  (found in most spice shelves)
½ tsp. salt
⅔ cup peanut oil (or olive oil)
¼ cup seasoned rice vinegar
  (found in Oriental foods
  section of most markets)
1 Tbsp. soy sauce
  (with equal amount of water)
¼ tsp. cayenne pepper
1 quarter-sized piece of
  sliced fresh ginger

PREPARATION:

Step 1:   Toast almonds in 275 degree oven for ½ hour.

Step 2:   Put almonds and rest of ingredients in blender and puree until smooth. Taste for additional seasoning. It should have a faint sweetness to it (seasoned rice vinegar has sugar in it). Thin with a little water if too thick.

Here are some of my favorite salads that may be used as a first course for a dinner party or as a lunch dish. The first three all use spinach greens instead of lettuce.

CHART HOUSE SPINACH SALAD

INGREDIENTS:

> ½ cup red wine vinegar
> 1½ teaspoons salt
> 1 tablespoon sugar
> ½ teaspoon dry mustard
> 1 rounded teaspoon minced sweet pickles
> ½ teaspoon chopped capers
> 1½ cups vegetable oil
> 1½ teaspoons olive oil
> 3 hard-cooked eggs, shredded
> 3 bunches spinach
> ¼ pound bacon, minced
> ½ small onion, minced
> ¼ pound mushrooms, sliced

PREPARATION:

Step 1: Blend together vinegar, salt, sugar, mustard, pickles and capers. Stir in vegetable and olive oils. Set aside.

Step 2: Clean spinach, removing tough stems. Drain on paper towels and pat dry. Place leaves in large bowl.

Step 3: Saute bacon until crisp. Remove bacon and sprinkle over spinach. Add onion and mushrooms to drippings in skillet. Saute until tender. Stir in 1 cup of reserved dressing. Bring to boil. Pour over spinach and toss. Garnish with shredded eggs. Serve with additional dressing.

Makes 4-6 servings.

SPINACH, CHICORY
AND GRAPEFRUIT SALAD

INGREDIENTS:

> ½ cup mayonnaise
> 3 tablespoons honey
> 2 tablespoons poppy seeds
> 1 tablespoon cider vinegar
> ¼ teaspoon salt
> ⅛ teaspoon ground red pepper
> 4 ounces fresh spinach
> ½ small head chicory
> 2 pink and/or white grapefruit, pared and sectioned
> 1 small red onion, thinly sliced

PREPARATION:

Step 1: In a small bowl, stir together mayonnaise, honey, poppy seeds, vinegar, salt and red pepper; cover and chill until ready to serve.

Step 2: Tear spinach and chicory into bite-size pieces; place in large bowl. Add grapefruit and onion. Just before serving, pour dressing over greens and gently toss to coat well.

Serves 6.

SPINACH SALAD WITH HOT BACON-CALVADOS DRESSING

INGREDIENTS:

2½ pounds fresh spinach leaves
2 small sweet red peppers, cored, seeded and cut into small strips
1 cup fresh mushrooms, thinly sliced
3 hard-cooked eggs, chopped
1 cup pine nuts, lightly toasted
Hot Bacon-Calvados Dressing

PREPARATION:

Step 1: Wash and pat dry spinach and remove stems. In large bowl, combine spinach with red-pepper strips, mushrooms, eggs, and pine nuts.

Step 2: Add hot dressing to taste, toss again to coat mixture lightly and serve at once.

Makes 6 servings.

HOT BACON-CALVADOS DRESSING

INGREDIENTS:

¼ pound bacon, diced
1 cup onion, diced
1 Granny Smith apple, peeled and thinly sliced
¼ cup Calvados (apple brandy) or other fruit brandy
¼ cup red wine vinegar
¼ cup apple cider
1 teaspoon cornstarch
¼ cup apple juice
1 clove garlic, crushed
Salt, pepper

PREPARATION:
Step 1: Cook bacon in skillet until crisp. Drain off fat. Add onion and apples to bacon; cook, stirring occasionally, until apples are tender. Stir in brandy. Add vinegar and cider and heat until mixture begins to simmer.
Step 2: Dissolve cornstarch in apple juice and add to skillet. Stir until mixture thickens slightly. Add garlic and season to taste with salt and pepper. Remove from heat but keep warm.
Makes about 1¾ cups.

ITALIAN CHOPPED SALAD

INGREDIENTS:
¼ head red cabbage
¼ head white cabbage
¼ head iceberg lettuce
5 slices dry salami
3 slices regular ham
12 pitted black olives
24 cooked garbanzo beans
Dressing

PREPARATION:
Step 1: Chop cabbages and lettuce as finely as possible. Dice salami, ham, and olives. Combine with garbanzo beans in large bowl.
Step 2: Pour on enough dressing to moisten salad (about 1 cup), or to taste. Toss and serve.
Makes 6-8 servings.

DRESSING
INGREDIENTS:
½ cup mayonnaise
2½ tablespoons red wine vinegar
1 teaspoon Dijon mustard
2 cups heavy (whipping) cream
Dash Worcestershire Sauce
Dash hot pepper sauce
Salt, pepper

PREPARATION:
To mayonnaise in bowl, add vinegar and mustard. Mix with whisk. Add cream, Worcestershire sauce, hot pepper sauce and season to taste with salt and pepper.
Makes 2½ cups.

MARINATED MUSHROOM SALAD

INGREDIENTS:

1 pound large white mushrooms
Juice of ½ lemon
2 tablespoons chopped parsley
2 tablespoons chopped chives
Vinaigrette
Sliced tomatoes

PREPARATION:

Step 1: Slice mushrooms and toss with lemon juice to prevent darkening. Add parsley, chives and Vinaigrette. Toss and chill.

Step 2: Toss again before serving. Garnish with a few tomato slices.

Makes 4 servings.

Note: For variation, use any onion, any cheese, or any vegetables, or a combination in salad.

VINAIGRETTE
INGREDIENTS:

3 tablespoons vinegar
2 tablespoons prepared mustard
1 cup oil
Dash wine
Salt, pepper

PREPARATION:

Blend together vinegar and mustard. Gradually add oil, pouring in thin stream and beating until mixture thickens slightly. Add wine. Season to taste with salt and pepper.

Makes about 1½ cups.

CURRIED EGG-CHICKEN-CANTALOUPE CUT-UP

INGREDIENTS:

1 medium cantaloupe, halved, peeled and seeded
⅓ cup mayonnaise
¼ cup plain low-fat yogurt
¾ teaspoon garlic salt
½ teaspoon curry powder

¼ teaspoon ground ginger
4 hard-cooked eggs, chopped
1 cup diced cooked chicken
⅓ cup chopped green onions, including tops
¼ cup chopped sweet green or red pepper
Thinly sliced sweet green or red
  peppers, optional
Hard-cooked egg wedges, optional

PREPARATION:
Step 1: Dice enough cantaloupe to make 1 cup. Set aside.
Step 2: Cut remaining cantaloupe into thin wedges for garnish, if desired. Refrigerate until just before serving.
Step 3: Blend mayonnaise, yogurt, garlic salt, curry powder and ginger in medium bowl. Toss with eggs, chicken, reserved 1 cup diced cantaloupe, onions and chopped pepper until evenly coated with dressing. Cover and chill to blend flavors.
Step 4: Just before serving, arrange reserved cantaloupe wedges in spoke fashion on large serving platter. Place pepper strips on each wedge. Spoon egg mixture into center and garnish with egg wedges.

Makes 4 servings.

24-HOUR SLAW

INGREDIENTS:
¾ cup sugar
1 large head cabbage, shredded
2 large red onions, thinly sliced
Hot Dressing

PREPARATION:
Step 1: Stir sugar into cabbage. Place half of cabbage in large bowl. Cover with onion slices. Top with remaining cabbage.
Step 2: Pour boiling Hot Dressing over slowly. Do not stir. Cover and refrigerate at once. Chill 24 hours. Stir well before serving.

Makes 8-10 servings.

HOT DRESSING
INGREDIENTS:
>1 teaspoon celery seeds
>1 teaspoon sugar
>1 teaspoon dry mustard
>1½ teaspoons salt
>1 cup cider vinegar
>1 cup oil

PREPARATION:
Step 1: Combine celery seeds, sugar, mustard, salt and vinegar in saucepan. Bring to rolling boil. Add oil, stirring, and return to rolling boil. Use HOT!

CRISPY MACARONI SALAD
INGREDIENTS:
>1 cup uncooked elbow macaroni
>Boiling salted water
>1 (1¼-ounce) envelope cheese sauce mix
>½ cup water
>¼ cup mayonnaise
>¼ cup sour cream
>½ teaspoon salt
>⅛ teaspoon black pepper
>2 cups finely shredded cabbage
>3 hard-cooked eggs, chopped
>½ cup chopped green pepper
>2 green onions, chopped

PREPARATION:
Step 1: Cook macaroni in boiling, salted water until tender. Drain and cool.
Step 2: Pour sauce mix into small saucepan and slowly stir in water. Heat just to boiling, stirring constantly.
Step 3: Stir in mayonnaise, sour cream, salt and pepper. Cool.
Step 4: Combine macaroni, cabbage, eggs, green pepper and green onions. Add sauce and toss to combine. Chill.

Makes 4-6 servings.

TEXAS POTATO SALAD

This is an unusual potato salad, and simple to make. I got the recipe from a little restaurant while driving from Houston to Galveston. Unlike most potato salads it is made with Idaho baking potatoes. Don't let the smoke barbecue sauce scare you off!

INGREDIENTS:
>5 medium large baking potatoes
>1 large red onion
>1 cup chopped celery
>½ cup of dill pickle juice
>¼ cup barbecue sauce
>Enough mayonnaise to bind salad together
>½ cup chopped parsley

PREPARATION:
Step 1: Scrub potatoes and place in pot of cold water to cover. Boil potatoes for 30 minutes or until fork tender. Drain in colander and let cool 15 minutes.

Step 2: Marinate chopped red onion and celery in pickle juice while potatoes cool.

Step 3: Peel potatoes and cut up into chunks. While they are still slightly warm add vegetables and juice. Add mayonnaise and barbecue sauce. Stir with wooden spoon and mix until everything is well integrated. Chill until ready to serve. Add ½ cup chopped parsley, stir again and serve.

I'm not too fond of molded salads, but this is one I rather enjoy.

AVOCADO MOLD WITH CRAB DRESSING

INGREDIENTS:
>1 6-oz. package lime gelatin
>2 cups hot water
>1 cup ice water
>½ tsp. salt
>2 Tbsp. lime juice
>¼ tsp. hot pepper sauce
>2 ripe avocados
>½ cup mayonnaise

½ cup sour cream
Crab dressing

PREPARATION:

Step 1: Dissolve gelatin in hot water. Stir in cold water, salt, lime juice and pepper sauce.

Step 2: Peel, pit and puree avocados. Add avocado, mayonnaise and sour cream to gelatin and beat with rotary beater.

Step 3: Pour mixture into 6 individual molds (spray molds lightly with non-stick spray) and chill until set. This takes about 3 to 4 hours to set properly. Unmold on cold plate and top with Crab Dressing.

CRAB DRESSING:

INGREDIENTS:

¾ cup mayonnaise
⅓ cup whole milk
1 cup sour cream
1½ tsp. lime juice
¼ tsp. paprika

PREPARATION:

Combine all of the above ingredients and mix well. Stir in 6 to 8 oz. crabmeat.

I'm not crazy about the old traditional Waldorf Salad, but here is a molded salad that does very nicely as an alternative.

OCTOBER SALAD MOLD

INGREDIENTS:

1 (3-ounce) package apple gelatin
1 cup boiling water
½ cup ice water
½ cup chopped pitted dates
1 cup diced red apples (unpeeled)
1 cup diced pears (unpeeled)
Ginger Salad Dressing

PREPARATION:

Step 1: Dissolve gelatin in boiling hot water. Add ice water. Chill until slightly thickened.

Step 2: Fold in fruits and pour into individual molds which have been sprayed lightly with non-stick spray. Chill until set. Serve with Ginger Salad Dressing.

GINGER SALAD DRESSING

Mix ⅓ cup mayonnaise with ½ cup sour cream. Fold in 2 Tbsps. minced candied ginger, 1½ Tbsps. honey mixed with 1 Tbsp. seasoned rice vinegar and 1 tsp. lemon juice. Put a dollop of dressing on each mold.

Now for what is perhaps my favorite salad of all. This is a variation on a traditional Chinese chicken salad.

CHINESE CHICKEN SALAD
(Advance Preparation Required)

INGREDIENTS:

2 whole chicken breasts (skinned and boned)
½ cup vegetable oil
2 Tbsps. lime juice
1 small white onion, chopped
3 Tbsps. white wine vinegar
1 crushed garlic clove
1 tsp. hot pepper sauce
3 individual packages of
    Top Ramen noodle soup
½ tsp. salt
¼ tsp. freshly ground black pepper
1 Tbsp. peanut oil
1 head iceberg lettuce, finely sliced
½ head of Chinese (Napa) cabbage,
    finely sliced
1 medium carrot, shredded
1 small sweet red papper (green may be
    used if red is unavailable)
1 cup fresh bean sprouts, coarsely chopped
2 bunches chopped green onions
    (tops included)
Chinese dressing (previously listed)

PREPARATION;

Step 1: Marinate chicken breasts **overnight** in mixture of vegetable oil, lime juice, chopped white onion, vinegar, garlic, pepper sauce, salt and pepper. Drain chicken and dice breasts in semi-small chunks.

Step 2:   Saute chicken in 1 Tbsp. peanut oil in hot skillet until chicken loses pink color. Do not overcook. Set chicken aside in covered bowl.

Step 3:   Put into large salad bowl the well-chilled vegetables and toss with chicken.

Step 4:   Remove the noodles from the soup packets (save the little broth packets to add to soups or gravies) and break them up, scattering them over salad. Pour dressing over all, toss lightly and serve at once so that noodles remain crisp.

A LITTLE SOMETHING FIRST:

When friends come to dinner it is customary to serve a cocktail or a glass of wine to help stimulate the appetite. It is also customary to serve some sort of appetizer to whet the palate with a promise of a good dinner to follow.

Unfortunately, these days most hosts try too hard and kill the appetite they hoped to stimulate. Please don't make the mistake of serving endless rounds of hors d'oeuvres (those are for cocktail parties) or you will suddenly find your guests pushing their food around the plate and feeling embarrassed because they simply are not hungry. As in all things, moderation is best.

Here are a few things I like to serve with drinks, and you will notice they do not include potato chips and dips or the ever popular salted peanuts...save those for munching in front of the T.V. set.

SALTED ALMONDS

If you can find whole blanched almonds all the better, but if not buy the whole unblanched almonds and pop them into boiling water for a minute or so. Rinse them off with cold water and the almonds will slip right out of the skins. Let them dry for half an hour on paper towels and they will be ready to fry.

In a medium sized saucepan heat three cups of any kind of non-saturated cooking oil over **moderately** high flame. After five minutes or so test the cooking temperature of the oil by dropping in an almond. If the oil is hot enough the almond will sizzle slightly.

Now add the almonds (one cup at a time) and stir constantly with a slotted spoon. When the almonds have turned a nice golden brown remove them quickly and put them on several thicknesses of paper toweling to drain. Salt them at once while they are still hot. Repeat the process until all almonds are fried. Let cool for half an hour and then store them in an airtight container. Before covering them put a crumpled up ball of wax paper over the top, then seal tightly. These will stay fresh for several weeks if unopened, and do save the oil in which the almonds were fried...it will have a delicate flavor that tastes slightly of the cooked nuts and is delicious in salad dressings or any food such as chicken, potatos, etc. that call for deep frying.

SPICY MACADAMIAS

We all know that the Macadamia nut is expensive but, when you are feeling in an extravagant mood, treat yourself to these wonderful nuts.

INGREDIENTS:
> Oil
> 2 small cloves of garlic, crushed
> 1 tsp. crushed dried chiles
> 1½ tsps. seasoned salt
> 1½ tsps. seasoned pepper
> 2 tsps. chili powder
> ¼ tsp. cayenne powder
> ¼ tsp. paprika
> ½ pound Macadamia nuts
> 1½ tsps. unsalted butter

PREPARATION:
Step 1: Rub heavy skillet with oil and place over moderate heat. Add all spices and stir briefly.
Step 2: Add Macadamia nuts and butter and reduce heat to low.
Step 3: Stir until nuts are coated with mixture, adding more butter if necessary.
Step 4: Cool in pan on rack, then store in tightly sealed container in cool place until ready to serve.

PICKLED SHRIMP

INGREDIENTS:

2½ lbs. medium large shrimp
¼ cup pickling spices
1 cup salad oil
¼ cup olive oil
1 cup white vinegar
2½ tsps. celery seed
2½ Tbsps. capers (plus a little of the juice)
Dash Tabasco
Salt to taste
2 very thinly sliced white onions

PREPARATION:

Step 1: Peel and devein shrimp. Bring six cups of water to fast boil and add pickling spices. Let boil a few minutes to release flavor of spices. Add shrimp and boil until just pink (2-3 min.)

Step 2: Drain shrimp, leaving whatever pickling spices remain in cooking pot.

Step 3: Mix together oils, vinegar, celery seed, capers, cayenne pepper, Tabasco, and salt to taste, to make marinade.

Step 4: In seal-tight container (large enough to hold shrimp) put in layer of shrimp, layer of onions, and some of marinade. Continue to layer ingredients in that order. Seal tightly and let sit for three days in refrigerator. This will keep for at least two weeks. Invert container every 24 hours and return to refrigerator. Drain well before serving.

GARLIC OLIVES

INGREDIENTS:

2 cups ripe green olives
4 cloves garlic, sliced
3 thin slices lemon
1 tsp. whole black peppercorns
3 bay leaves
1 tsp. each dried thyme and basil
¼ cup sherry
Olive oil

PREPARATION:

Step 1: Combine olives, garlic, lemon slices, herbs, peppercorns and sherry in a jar. Add oil to cover.

Step 2: Marinate 3 days to blend flavors. Drain and serve in relish dish.

WARM BRIE

INGREDIENTS:

1 six- to eight-inch round Brie cheese
¼ cup chopped pecans
¼ cup crumbled Bleu cheese
2 Tbsps. minced scallions
Sweet butter

PREPARATION:

Step 1: Saute pecans in sweet butter until lightly browned.

Step 2: Slice unpeeled Brie laterally to make two round halves. This is best done while Brie is still cold and firm.

Step 3: Sprinkle bottom half of cheese (skin side down) with pecans, Bleu cheese and scallions. Cover with top half of Brie (skin side up).

Step 4: Place cheese in small round oven-proof dish and bake at 350° 4 to 5 mins. until cheese is soft.

Serve with English Water Crackers.

CHEESE MERINGUES

These are particularly good for dieters, and a fine way to use up left over egg whites.

INGREDIENTS:

3 egg whites (room temperature) beaten stiff
3 Tbsps. freshly grated Parmesan cheese
½ tsp. cayenne pepper

PREPARATION:

Fold egg whites, cheese, and pepper carefully together. Drop 1½ to 2 Tbsp. rounds of mixture on ungreased cookie sheet. Bake in a pre-heated 350° oven until light brown. Remove meringues with spatula and serve warm.

CHEESE CRISPS

INGREDIENTS:

½ cup softened sweet (unsalted) butter
2 cups shredded sharp Cheddar cheese
1½ cups flour
½ tsps. salt
¼ tsps. dry mustard
Dash cayenne pepper

PREPARATION:

Step 1: Cream butter and cheese together until light and fluffy.

Step 2: Sift together flour, salt, mustard and cayenne.

Step 3: Add flour mixture to butter-cheese mixture and blend well. Shape dough into a roll about 1½ inches in diameter. Wrap in waxed paper and chill for 1 hour.

Step 4: Slice thinly and bake slices on cookie sheet at 400°; 10 to 12 mins.

ENTREES
(BEEF)

And now we come to the more difficult part of dinner. **THE MAIN COURSE!!** This is the time that one does a lot of praying in the kitchen, comes to the table and waits for the first guest to say "Marvelous". If no one says anything, pretend to have a fainting spell and ask to be taken to the nearest emergency hospital. This will generate a lot of sympathy, and everything that went wrong can be blamed on poor health.

These recipes are guaranteed to elicit "oohs" and "aahs" from your guests or family. Just sit there humbly and never say things like "It was better the last time I made it" or "Just lucky, I guess". Believe me, half the people I have cooked for are so grateful to eat something that wasn't a frozen dinner their compliments are profuse.

The next recipes will deal mostly with meat so if you have any friends who come to dinner and make the surprise statement, "We've turned vegetarian!", simply smile and remark "The hell you say!"

First we'll start with beef dishes. Everything from roasts to stews to meat loaves... even two recipes for oxtails (I can hear you say "Ugh!", but give them a try).

The accompanying vegetable and potatoes are up to you, although I will give a few recipes later in the book for the more unusual side dishes.

Some of these recipes are simple and some more complicated, but if you follow the directions you will find even the more difficult ones can be fun. Cooking can be a great tension reliever, so smile and enjoy it all.

PARTY BRISKET
(Advance Preparation Required)

INGREDIENTS:

> 1 (5-6 pound) beef brisket
> 2 large onions
> 2 teaspoons salt
> 2 teaspoons celery salt
> Pungent Sauce
> Brisket Broth

PREPARATION:
Step 1: Place brisket in roaster or Dutch oven and cover with water.
Step 2: Peel onions, score at top, and add to brisket.
Step 3: Add salt and celery salt. Bring to full boil and skim.
Step 4: Reduce heat, cover and simmer 3 hours (if using roaster, cook over 2 burners).
Step 5: Remove meat, drain (reserving liquid for broth) and cool.
Step 6: Brush with Pungent Sauce. Cover and refrigerate overnight.
Step 7: To serve, slice desired amount of brisket, cutting across grain. Lay slices in Dutch oven and add 1 cup Brisket Broth. Cover and bake at 250-300° 1 hour.
Makes 8-10 servings.

PUNGENT SAUCE:
INGREDIENTS:
2 dashes bottled onion juice
1 dash bottled garlic juice
1 teaspoon coarse black pepper
1 teaspoon instant coffee powder
2 tablespoons brown sugar
2 tablespoons Worcestershire sauce
½ cup catsup

PREPARATION:
Step 1: Combine all ingredients and mix well.
Makes about ¾ cup.

BRISKET BROTH:
INGREDIENTS:
Broth from cooked brisket
1 bunch carrots, cut diagonally in large chunks
1 bunch celery, cut diagonally in large slices
2-3 tablespoons chopped parsley
1 leek, white part only, sliced
5 bouillon cubes
1 cup water

PREPARATION:
Step 1: Let broth stand overnight in refrigerator. Skim off fat and discard.
Step 2: Place broth in kettle. Add carrots and celery (including leaves), parsley and leek.
Step 3: Dissolve bouillon cubes in water and add to broth. Cover and simmer over low heat 1 hour.

Step 4: Use 1 cup broth to reheat brisket slices. Serve remainder with vegetables or strain and serve vegetables separately. Strained broth may be used as base for other soups.

GERMAN-STYLE BRISKET

INGREDIENTS:
> 2 tablespoons oil
> 1 (3½-4 pound) beef brisket
> 1 (10½ ounce) can condensed French onion soup
> ½ cup vinegar
> 2 medium bay leaves
> ¼ teaspoon black pepper
> ⅛ teaspoon ground cloves
> 6 small potatoes, cut into chunks
> 3 medium carrots, cut into chunks
> 3 medium parsnips, cut into ¼ inch strips
> ½ cup finely crushed gingersnaps

PREPARATION:
Step 1: Heat oil in 6-quart Dutch oven over medium-high heat. Brown roast in oil on all sides, then spoon off fat.
Step 2: Stir in soup, vinegar, bay leaves, pepper and cloves. Reduce heat to low and simmer, covered, 2 hours.
Step 3: Add potatoes and simmer, covered, 30 minutes longer.
Step 4: Add carrots and parsnips and simmer, covered, until roast and vegetables are fork-tender, about 30 minutes.
Step 5: Remove roast and vegetables to serving platter. Remove bay leaves and skim off fat.
Step 6: Stir in gingersnaps, stirring to desired consistency. Serve gravy over roast and vegetables.

Makes 10-12 servings.

BURGUNDY BEEF
(Advance Preparation Required)

INGREDIENTS:
> 5 lbs. beef chuck roast, cut into 1½ inch cubes
> Flour
> Butter
> ¼ teaspoon pepper

                    ¼ cup cognac
                    2¼ ounces meat extract
                    ½ pound bacon (diced)
                    4 garlic cloves (minced)
                    2 carrots, coarsely chopped
                    2 cups chopped onions
                    1 tablespoon snipped parsley
                    2 bay leaves
                    1 teaspoon thyme
                    1¼ cups Burgundy wine
                    1 cup sweet sherry
                    1 pound small white onions
                    Sugar
                    2 pounds fresh mushrooms
                    2 teaspoons lemon juice

PREPARATION: (Day Before)
Step 1: Roll beef in flour, brown well in ¼ cup butter in Dutch
         oven. Sprinkle on cognac and ignite. Stir in meat
         extract.
Step 2: Heat oven to 350°. Add all ingredients except small
         onions, sugar, mushrooms and lemon juice.
Step 3: Bake covered, 2-2½ hours. When meat is tender, put
         vegetables and gravy through food mill. If you don't have
         a food mill, use the blender, or force the vegetables and
         gravy through a strainer. Pour over meat and re-
         frigerate.

Before Serving:
         Brown small onions in hot butter, then sprinkle with sugar
         and ½ cup Burgundy. Cook, covered, 15 minutes. Add
         water, if necessary. Add to meat with liquid and 1 tables-
         poon of sugar. In 2 tablespoons butter, saute mushrooms
         till brown on one side. Turn, sprinkle with lemon juice and
         add to meat mixture.

Serves 12-16 people.

BEEF CURRY

INGREDIENTS:
                    1 onion
                    ¼ cup green pepper, chopped
                    ½ cup celery, chopped
                    4 tablespoons butter
                    1½ pounds lean beef, coarsely ground

1 clove finely chopped garlic
¼ cup flour
2 cups beef stock or condensed beef broth
2 tablespoons curry powder
Salt, pepper, MSG (optional) to taste
Chutney Sauce

PREPARATION:

Step 1: Saute onion, green pepper, celery in butter. Add chopped beef and brown lightly, with garlic.

Step 2: Stir in flour; add beef stock, curry powder, salt, pepper and MSG. Cook briefly (5-10 minutes) until tender. Serve over cooked brown rice and top with Chutney Sauce.

CHUTNEY SAUCE:
INGREDIENTS:
½ cup coarsely chopped celery
¼ cup coarsely chopped green pepper
2 tablespoons butter
2 small tomatoes (peeled, seeded, and chopped)
¼ cup cider vinegar
2 tablespoons sugar
Dash cayenne pepper

PREPARATION:
Saute celery and green pepper in butter; add tomatoes, vinegar, sugar, and cayenne. Cook and stir to tender consistency and nice sweet-sour taste.

Serves 4-6.

BARBECUED
SPICY-SWEET RIBS

INGREDIENTS:
3 pounds beef ribs or short ribs
¼ cup soy sauce
1 tablespoon minced garlic
2 teaspoons grated orange peel
2 teaspoons minced ginger root
¼ teaspoon black pepper
Honey Baste

PREPARATION:

Step 1: Trim excess fat from bottom and sides of ribs. Lightly score top side of ribs.

Step 2: Combine soy sauce, garlic, orange peel, ginger and pepper and pour over ribs in shallow dish.

Step 3: Refrigerate, covered, 8 hours or overnight, turning occasionally.

Step 4: Place ribs on grill 4-5 inches above medium-low coals. Place cover on grill and cook ribs 15-18 minutes, turning and basting frequently with remaining marinade.

Step 5: Brush ribs with Honey Baste during last 10-15 minutes of cooking time. Continue cooking 2-3 minutes or to desired degree of doneness.

Makes 6 servings.

HONEY BASTE:

COMBINE:

> ¼ cup honey
> 1 tablespoon soy sauce
> 1 tablespoon hot, dry mustard
> 1 tablespoon lemon juice

Use to brush over barbecued meat.

AMBASSADOR HOTEL
BEEF SHORT RIBS

INGREDIENTS:

> 6 (12-ounce) beef short ribs (4½ pounds)
> Salt, pepper & rosemary
> 1 cup diced celery
> 1 cup diced carrots
> ½ cup red wine
> Brown Gravy

PREPARATION:

Step 1: Sprinkle each rib with salt, pepper and rosemary to taste. Place in baking pan with celery and carrots. Bake at 350° 1 hour.

Step 2: Add red wine and Brown Gravy. Cover with foil and bake 1½ hours or until meat is tender when fork is inserted.

Makes 6 servings.

BROWN GRAVY

INGREDIENTS:

6 tablespoons butter
6 tablespoons flour
1 (14½ ounce) can clear chicken broth
1 (14½ ounce) can clear beef broth
1 tablespoon beef concentrate powder
Salt, pepper

PREPARATION:

Melt butter and stir in flour until smooth and pale gold. Stir in chicken broth, beef broth and beef concentrate until blended. Bring to boil and simmer 10 minutes. Season to taste with salt and pepper if needed.

GRILLED STEAK WITH GREEN-PEPPERCORN SAUCE

INGREDIENTS:

1 3-pound sirloin steak, cut 2 inches thick
Salt, pepper
Green-Peppercorn Sauce

PREPARATION:

Step 1: Place steak on rack in shallow baking pan. Roast at 400° 10-12 minutes per side for rare; 12-15 minutes per side for medium rare; and 15-18 minutes per side for well done. (For best results, use a meat thermometer and undercook a few degrees.) Turn only once. Season to taste with salt and pepper after turning.

Step 2: When steak is done, remove from heat and place in warm spot for about 10 minutes to let juices set.

Step 3: To serve, carve across grain in thin slices, allowing 2-3 slices per serving. Serve Green-Peppercorn Sauce separately.

Makes 6-10 servings.

GREEN-PEPPERCORN SAUCE

INGREDIENTS:

1 cup beef stock, preferably unsalted
½ cup brandy
½ cup heavy (whipping) cream
2 tablespoons green peppercorns
½ cup butter or margarine
Salt, pepper

PREPARATION:
Step 1: Combine stock, brandy and cream in saucepan and bring to boil, stirring frequently. Boil until reduced by about half.
Step 2: Stir in peppercorns with a dash of their pickling juice.
Step 3: Cut butter into 4-6 pieces. Remove pan from heat and, with wire whisk, beat in butter pieces, one at a time, until sauce is smooth. Season to taste with salt and pepper. Makes about 1½ cups sauce.

Note: For a thicker sauce, blend 1 teaspoon cornstarch with about 2 tablespoons sauce before butter is whisked in. Stir mixture into rest of sauce and cook 2 minutes, then whisk in butter.

FRIED FLANK STEAK

INGREDIENTS:
2 pounds flank steak, tenderized
  once by butcher
½ cup brown sugar, packed
½ cup soy sauce
1 teaspoon garlic powder
1 teaspoon ground ginger
5 eggs, beaten
1 bunch green onion tops, chopped
Cornstarch
Oil

PREPARATION:
Step 1: Cut steak into bite-size pieces.
Step 2: In large bowl, stir together brown sugar, soy sauce, garlic powder and ginger. Add flank steak and marinate 15 minutes.
Step 3: Combine eggs and green onions in medium bowl.
Step 4: Place cornstarch in separate bowl.
Step 5: Dip each piece of meat lightly into cornstarch, then into beaten eggs and green onions.
Step 6: Heat ½ inch oil in medium size skillet. Fry meat in hot oil until golden brown, turning once. Drain on paper towels and serve.
Makes 6-8 servings.

KOREAN BARBECUED BEEF

INGREDIENTS:

          2 pounds sirloin steak
          (or use short-rib or flank steak)
          3 green onions, chopped
          1 small onion, chopped
          3 cloves garlic, crushed
          5 tablespoons soy sauce
          1-2 tablespoons dry Sherry
          Salt and 1/8 teaspoon black pepper, or to taste
          1/4 cup sliced mushrooms
          1/4 cup sugar
          2 tablespoons sesame oil

PREPARATION:

Step 1: Slice steak very thin (partially freeze meat for ease in slicing).

Step 2: Combine green onions, onion, garlic, soy cause, Sherry, salt to taste, pepper, mushrooms, sugar and sesame oil.

Step 3: Marinate meat in mixture several hours.

Step 4: Cook on grill 5-8 minutes or until done, turning occasionally. Serve hot.

Makes about 6 servings.

SPICY POT ROAST

INGREDIENTS:

          4-5 lb. beef pot roast
          1/4 cup shortening
          3 cups water
          1 cup vinegar
          1/2 cup firmly packed brown sugar
          1/2 cup chopped onion
          2 Tablespoons mixed pickling spices
          2 teaspoons cardamom seed
          1/3 cup flour
          1/3 cup cold water

PREPARATION:

Step 1: In Dutch oven or heavy skillet, brown meat slowly on all sides in the shortening. Pour off excess fat.

Step 2: Add next six ingredients. Simmer, covered, 3-4 hours or until meat is tender.

Step 3: Remove meat; keep warm.

Strain stock. Measure 4 cups. Blend flour and the ⅓ cup cold water; add to measured stock. Cook, stirring, until thickened.
Yield: 8 portions.

IRISH BEEF STEW

INGREDIENTS:

>2 pounds beef round, cut into 1 inch cubes
>1½ tablespoon flour
>1 teaspoon salt
>½ teaspoon dry mustard
>¼ teaspoon pepper
>2 tablespoons oil
>1 (10½ ounce) can beef broth
>Water
>1 teaspoon sugar
>1 bay leaf
>1 sprig parsley
>Pinch thyme
>3 carrots, cut into chunks
>1 white turnip, cut into chunks
>2 onions, quartered
>4 stalks celery, cut into 1½ inch lengths
>2 tomatoes, peeled and sliced
>2 tablespoons cornstarch
>Duchess Potatoes

PREPARATION:
Step 1: Coat beef with flour mixed with salt, mustard and pepper. Brown quickly in oil. Stir in remaining seasoned flour.
Step 2: Add broth and water to make 2 cups liquid. Add sugar, bay leaf, parsley and thyme. Cover and simmer about 1½ hours or until beef is tender.
Step 3: Add carrots, turnip and onions. Top with celery and tomatoes. Cover and cook an additional 10 minutes.
Step 4: Remove bay leaf and parsley.
Step 5: Mix cornstarch with 2 tablespoons cold water. Stir into stew and cook a few minutes longer, stirring gently occasionally. Serve with Duchess Potatoes.
Makes 6 servings.

DUCHESS POTATOES
INGREDIENTS:

      2 cups mashed potatoes
      2 egg yolks
      2 tablespoons milk
      Melted butter

PREPARATION:

Step 1: Combine mashed potatoes, egg yolks, milk and 2 tablespoons butter. Beat until smooth. Turn into pastry bag fitted with star tip. Press out into 6 rosettes onto greased baking sheet.
(If no pastry bag is available, make 6 mounds of the mixture and use the top of a knife or spoon to press each mound into a pleasing pattern. They won't look quite as pretty, but they'll taste just as good.)

Step 2: Brush potatoes with melted butter. Broil until heated through and lightly browned.

Makes 6 servings.

FANCIER NOT SO IRISH STEW

INGREDIENTS:

      2½ pounds beef stew meat
      3 tablespoons seasoned flour (see
        "Irish Beef Stew" for seasonings)
      1½ tablespoons butter
      1½ tablespoons olive oil
      2 tablespoons sweet paprika
      1 teaspoon black pepper (coarse grind)
      1 carrot (finely chopped)
      1 onion (finely chopped)
      1 clove garlic, finely chopped
      ½ can good beer
      2 cans beef broth
      2 cans water (use beef broth can to measure)
      1 bay leaf
      1 teaspoon thyme
      2 large carrots (sliced diagonally into chunks)
      1 turnip (cubed)
      2 stalks celery (sliced diagonally)
      2 tablespoons chopped parsley
      4 medium White Rose potatoes
        (cut into chunks)

1 medium can Mexican-style tomatoes
(break up)
½ jar Ortega chili salsa (med. hot)
1 can beef gravy (Franco-American)
1½ cups quartered mushrooms
½ head of chopped cabbage
½ green pepper (chopped)
3 tablespoons soft butter
3 rounded tablespoons flour
1 (10 oz) package frozen peas
1-2 sliced zucchini (depending on size)

PREPARATION:

Step 1: Toss beef cubes in seasoned flour. Heat butter and olive oil in heavy Dutch oven, add beef and brown on all sides.

Step 2: Stir in paprika and pepper, and stir until nicely browned.

Step 3: Add chopped carrot, onion, garlic, and green pepper and stir until vegetables soften and brown slightly.

Step 4: Add beer, beef broth, water, bay leaf, thyme, and cabbage. Bring to boil and simmer over low flame 1½ hours in partially-covered kettle. Stir occasionally.

Step 5: Add carrots, turnip, celery, mushrooms, parsley, potatoes, tomatoes, salsa, and gravy. Simmer 1 more hour (partially covered).

Step 6: Mix together soft butter & 3 Tbsp. flour, stir into stew when it comes to a bubble.

Step 7: Add peas and zucchini and simmer another 15 minutes.

Serves 6.

ONTRA BRAISED OX JOINTS

INGREDIENTS:

2 pounds oxtails
¼ cup celery slices
2 tablespoons instant chopped onion, rehydrated, or ¼ cup chopped onion
¼ teaspoon granulated garlic or 1 clove garlic, minced
½ teaspoon paprika
¼ cup flour
¼ cup tomato sauce

⅛ teaspoon EACH ground thyme,
    marjoram, dry mustard, celery salt
1½ teaspoons beef stock base
2 cups boiling water
Salt, pepper
1-2 tablespoons dry red wine

PREPARATION:

Step 1: Place oxtails in roasting pan and roast uncovered at 350°
about 1 hour or until golden brown. Turn occasionally.
Remove from oven and skim off fat.

Step 2: Add celery, onion and garlic and return to oven for about
30 minutes. Again, skim off fat.

Step 3: Stir paprika and flour into pan drippings. Add tomato
sauce, thyme, marjoram, mustard and celery salt.

Step 4: Dissolve beef base in boiling water and stir into stew,
blending well. Season to taste with salt and pepper.
Cover, return to oven and cook about 1 hour or until
meat is tender.

Step 5: Remove from oven and correct seasonings, if necessary.
Stir in wine.

Makes 4 servings.

GRANDMA'S OXTAILS

INGREDIENTS:
2 pounds oxtails
2 quarts cold water
1 tsp. Chinese five-spice powder
1 stick cinnamon
¼ teaspoon MSG (optional)
2 tablespoons brown sugar
3 tablespoons soy sauce

PREPARATION:

Step 1: Put oxtails in large kettle, cover with water and bring to a
boil. Simmer for about 5 minutes. Drain and rinse oxtails.
(This eliminates scum that can cloud finished sauce.)

Step 2: Put oxtails back in kettle and add 2 quarts water, 5-spice
powder, and cinnamon. Cover and bring to boil. Reduce
heat and simmer gently about 1 hour.

Step 3: Add MSG, brown sugar and soy sauce. Cover and continue simmering for 2 additional hours.

Step 4: Remove oxtails to serving platter. Turn heat up high and boil sauce down to about 1 cup. The sauce will thicken to a rich delicious glaze. Pour sauce over oxtails.

YANKS CAJUN MEAT LOAF

INGREDIENTS:

½ cup chopped green onions
1 cup finely diced red, green or yellow pepper
1 cup diced onions
¼ cup diced celery
2 small jalapeno chiles
¼ cup unsalted butter
½ teaspoon cayenne pepper
1¼ tablesooons hot pepper sauce
1¼ tablespoons Worcestershire sauce
2 bay leaves
2 tablespoons to ¼ cup Cajun spices
(bottled blend)*
⅓ cup milk
⅓ cup Heinz 57 sauce
⅓ cup catsup
1 pound ground beef (80% lean, 20% fat)
¾ pound ground pork
2 large eggs, lightly beaten
¾ cup bread crumbs

PREPARATION:

Step 1: Sauce green onions, pepper, onions, celery and jalapenos in butter until tender, about 10 minutes.

Step 2: Add cayenne, hot pepper sauce, Worcestershire, bay leaves and Cajun spices. Saute 5 minutes longer.

Step 3: Add milk, Heinz 57 sauce and catsup. Simmer 5 minutes. Remove from heat, discard bay leaves, then add beef, pork, eggs and crumbs. Mix well.

Step 4: Pack mixture into 9×5-inch glass loaf pan. Cover with foil. Bake in pan of hot water at 350° for ½ hour. Remove cover and bake additional 30 minutes.

Step 5: Remove from oven and let stand 10 minutes before slicing.

Makes 6-8 servings.

*Or make your own Cajun spice mixture:

Mix together:

> 1 Tbsp. salt
> ¾ tsp. cayenne pepper
> 1 tsp. black pepper
> ½ tsp. white pepper
> ½ tsp. ground cumin
> ½ tsp. ground nutmeg
> ½ tsp. sweet paprika

ITALIAN ROLLED MEAT LOAF

INGREDIENTS:

> Sauce
> 2 pounds ground beef
> ½ pound ground lean pork
> 1½ cups Italian-style seasoned bread crumbs
> ½ cup grated Parmesan cheese
> ½ teaspoon garlic salt
> ½ teaspoon black pepper
> 1 rounded teaspoon oregano
> ¼ teaspoon salt
> ½ cup cold water
> 3 eggs
> ¼ pound thinly sliced Genoa or hard salami
> 1 6-ounce can pitted ripe black olives, sliced

PREPARATION:

Step 1: Prepare and simmer sauce.

Step 2: In a large bowl, mix beef, pork, bread crumbs, Parmesan cheese, garlic salt, pepper, oregano, salt, water and eggs. Mix thoroughly by hand. Place mixture on sheet of waxed paper and press out into a rectangle, about 18×11 inches. Cover the surface with slices of salami, keeping the salami about ½ inch away from edges. Top with sliced olives. Roll up from shorter edge, pinching and patting sides and ends to give an unbroken surface.

Step 3: Place loaf in lightly greased 12×7-inch dish and bake at 500° 15 minutes.

Step 4: Remove and cool a few minutes, spooning off any fat.

Step 5: Pour the hot sauce over. Cover with foil and bake at 350° 45 minutes.

Step 6: Turn off oven and let loaf sit for ½ hour, covered.

Step 7: Remove the meat loaf roll, slice and serve.

Step 8: Stir the sauce well and put a tablespoon or more over each slice. Enough sauce will be left to serve with any pasta.

Makes 8-10 servings.

SAUCE:

INGREDIENTS:

2 tablespoons olive oil
2 cloves garlic, crushed
1 28-ounce can Italian-style peeled tomatoes, blender chopped
1 28-ounce can tomato puree
1 16-ounce can tomato paste
2 teaspoons basil
½ teaspoon thyme
1 teaspoon ground coriander
½ teaspoon salt
1 teaspoon pepper
1 cup chianti wine
3 tablespoons grated Parmesan cheese

PREPARATION:

Step 1: Heat oil and saute garlic lightly. Add Italian tomatoes, tomato puree and tomato paste. Stir gently. Add basil, thyme, coriander, salt, pepper and wine. Heat to boiling.

Step 2: Sprinkle with Parmesan cheese and simmer, stirring frequently while preparing the meat loaf roll.

TAMALE PIE

INGREDIENTS:

¾ pound ground beef
1 chorizo, chopped
1 cup chopped onion
½ cup chopped celery
1 cup sliced, pitted ripe olives
1 (16-ounce) can cream-style corn
2 cups canned tomatoes, broken up
1 tablespoon chili powder
1 teaspoon salt
½ teaspoon garlic salt
Cornmeal Crust

PREPARATION:
Step 1: Brown beef and chorizo over medium heat and drain thoroughly.
Step 2: Add onion, celery, olives, corn, tomatoes, chili powder, salt, and garlic salt. Cover and cook over low heat, 15 minutes.
Step 3: Line a greased 2½-quart casserole with half of the Cornmeal Crust mixture. Add meat filling. Top with remaining cornmeal mixture. Bake at 375° for 40 minutes.
Makes 6 servings.

CORNMEAL CRUST

INGREDIENTS:
1 cup yellow cornmeal
½ teaspoon chili powder
1½ teaspoons salt
1 (13-ounce) can evaporated milk
1¼ cups water

PREPARATION:
Mix cornmeal, chili powder and salt in a saucepan. Gradually stir in evaporated milk and water. Cook and stir over low heat until mixture thickens but is not too thick, about 10 minutes. Mixture will continue to thicken after it is removed from heat and should be used immediately.

SWEET-SOUR CABBAGE ROLLS

INGREDIENTS:
1 cup partially cooked rice
½ pound ground beef chuck
1 pound ground veal or lamb
1 teaspoon salt
⅛ teaspoon pepper
1 small onion, minced
1 large head cabbage
Boiling salted water
Beef stock (or water)

1 small onion
6 whole cloves
1 bay leaf
3 tablespoons lemon juice
2 tablespoons brown sugar
2 tablespoons tomato paste
½ cup raisins
8 or 9 gingersnaps, crushed

PREPARATION:

Step 1: Combine rice, meats, salt, pepper and onion and mix lightly. Carefully cut core from cabbage and remove leaves so they do not break. Drop a few at a time into boiling salted water and cook 7-8 minutes or until just wilted.

Step 2: Place generous tablespoonful of meat mixture on each leaf at rib end. Roll, turning in sides of leaf and roll to make a neat cylinder. Secure with wood picks or tie.

Step 3: Place rolls in deep kettle and cover with beef stock. Stud remaining onion with cloves and add to kettle along with bay leaf, lemon juice, sugar and tomato paste. Cover and simmer 1 hour.

Step 4: Add raisins and crushed gingersnaps and simmer 15 minutes, stirring occasionally.

Step 5: Arrange cooked cabbage rolls in a single layer in a 3-4 inch deep baking pan.

Step 6: Check sauce for seasoning, adding salt and more lemon juice or sugar for desired sweet-sour flavor. Remove bay leaf and onions from sauce, pour over rolls and bake at 375° 30-40 minutes or until sauce is thick and rolls are browned.

Makes 6-8 servings.

MOUSSAKA

INGREDIENTS:

2 medium eggplants
Salt
1 pound ground beef
2 tablespoons butter
1½ teaspoons Greek seasoning
1 medium onion, finely chopped
1 clove garlic, minced
Dash cinnamon

¼ teaspoon ground nutmeg
1 tablespoon chopped parsley
½ cup mashed Italian plum tomatoes
¼ cup red wine
Oil
¼ cup grated Romano cheese
Cheese Sauce

PREPARATION:

Step 1: Peel and slice eggplants length-wise into ¼-inch slices. Sprinkle with salt and set aside on paper towels to absorb moisture.

Step 2: Prepare meat sauce. Saute ground beef in butter with Greek seasoning, onion and garlic, crumbling meat until browned. Add cinnamon, nutmeg, parsley and tomatoes and stir well. Add wine, cover and simmer 30 minutes.

Step 3: Rinse salted eggplant and pat dry with paper towels. Lightly oil skillet and fry eggplant over very high heat until golden. Drain on paper towels.

Step 4: In greased 9×9-inch baking pan, place layer of eggplant and top with meat mixture. Sprinkle with grated Romano cheese. Continue layering ingredients in same order until all are used, ending with eggplant.

Step 5: Pour Cheese Sauce over all. Bake at 375° 45 minutes to 1 hour.

Step 6: Let stand 15 minutes to set before slicing into 3-inch squares.

Makes 6 servings.

CHEESE SAUCE

INGREDIENTS:

2 egg yolks
1 cup milk
½ cup grated Romano cheese

PREPARATION:

Beat egg yolks until frothy. Add milk and cheese, mixing well.

MY FAVORITE TEXAS CHILI

INGREDIENTS:

¼ cup oil
4 pounds top round, cut into ½-inch cubes
6 cloves garlic, ground or minced
2 large green peppers, chopped
2 large onions, chopped
1 (¾-ounce) jar cumin
¼ cup oregano
2 bay leaves
2 tablespoons crushed dried red chiles,
  or to taste
3 tablespoons flour
1 quart beef stock
⅔ cup tomato paste
Hot pepper sauce
Salt
Beans
Sour Cream
Shredded Cheese

PREPARATION:

Step 1: Heat oil over medium heat. Add beef and sear well. Remove meat and put aside.

Step 2: Add garlic, peppers and onions and saute over medium-low heat for 10 minutes. Add cumin, oregano, bay leaves and chiles. Stir and mix well. Add flour and mix well. Cook 10 minutes over medium-low heat until smooth paste is golden brown.

Step 3: Add beef and stir in beef stock, tomato paste and hot pepper sauce to taste. Bring to boil, reduce heat and simmer, covered 30-45 minutes or until meat is done.

Step 4: Season to taste with salt. Serve with beans (recipe on next page) on side along with sour cream and shredded cheese.

Makes 8-10 servings.

BEANS

INGREDIENTS:

1 pound dry pinto beans
Water
3 or 4 strips pork skins or 4- to 6-ounce knuckles
    or pigs feet
2 green peppers, chopped
1 large onion, chopped
2 cloves garlic, minced
1 tablespoon crushed dried red chiles
Hot pepper sauce
½ cup tomato paste
Salt

PREPARATION:

Step 1: Soak beans overnight in water to cover. Strain.

Step 2: Cook beans with pork skins (or knuckles) in fresh water until beans are just done, about 45-50 minutes. Discard pork skins.

Step 3: Add peppers, onion, garlic, red chiles and hot pepper sauce to taste, stirring to blend. Bring to boil, reduce heat, cover and simmer over low heat until beans are tender, about 20-30 minutes. Stir in tomato paste, mixing well. Season to taste with salt.

Makes 8-10 servings.

ENTREES
(CHICKEN AND TURKEY)

Everyone has thousands of recipes for chicken, but here are a few more for your collection. And do try the Nicaraguan Turkey — it's a humdinger!

This first recipe is so simple you won't believe it — but it's good!

BAKED CHICKEN VERA

INGREDIENTS:

        1 cut-up frying chicken
        1 can cream of mushroom soup (undiluted)
        1 tablespoon butter
        2 tablespoons dehydrated onion flakes
        ¼ cup fresh chopped parsley
        1 tablespoon paprika

PREPARATION:

Step 1:   Place chicken in 2-quart glass casserole with butter.
Step 2:   Sprinkle chicken with onion flakes, parsley, and paprika. Cover all with mushroom soup.
Step 3:   Cover casserole and bake at 275° for 2 hours.

Serves 3-4

CHICKEN WITH FRESH LEMON SAUCE

INGREDIENTS:

        3 pounds boned chicken breasts
        1 tablespoon sherry
        1 tablespoon soy sauce
        1 teaspoon salt
        1 teaspoon minced ginger
        ½ teaspoon sugar
        1 cup flour
        ½ cup cornstarch
        1 teaspoon baking powder
        1½-2 cups cold water
        Oil
        Lemon Sauce

PREPARATION:

Step 1:   Cut chicken breasts into bite-size pieces, 1-½×¾×¼-inch. Combine sherry, soy sauce, ½ teaspoon salt, ginger and sugar. Mix with chicken and marinate for 5 minutes.

Step 2: Combine flour, cornstarch, ½ teaspoon salt and baking powder. Add water and 2 teaspoons oil and mix to make a batter. Dip chicken pieces in batter and fry in deep oil heated to 350° for 5-7 minutes or until golden brown. Drain and serve with Lemon Sauce.

LEMON SAUCE
INGREDIENTS:

2 tablespoons oil
1 tablespoon ginger, crushed
1 clove garlic, crushed
2 lemons, thinly sliced
Sugar
2 cups chicken broth
½ cup lemon juice
Salt
1 tablespoon sherry
Grated peel of 1 lemon
2½ tablespoons cornstarch
3 tablespoons water
(Optional: Deep fried rice sticks, more lemon slices)

PREPARATION:
Step 1: Heat oil, add ginger and garlic and cook until browned. Add lemon slices and stir fry ½ to 1 minute. Sprinkle with ½ teaspoon sugar and remove from pan.
Step 2: Add chicken broth, lemon juice, ⅓ cup sugar, salt to taste (start with ¼ teaspoon), sherry and lemon peel to pan. Blend cornstarch with water and stir into broth mixture. Cook and stir until thickened.
Step 3: Taste and add more sugar or lemon juice if needed. Add lemon slices to sauce and pour over chicken.

Optional:
If desired, arrange a border of deep-fried rice sticks around a serving platter. Stand halved lemon slices inside the rice sticks and place chicken and sauce in center.

Serves 6.

SPECIAL BAKED CHICKEN

INGREDIENTS:

4 (6-ounce) chicken breast halves,
boned and skinned
¼ teaspoon salt

¼ teaspoon black pepper
1 cup sliced, sauteed mushrooms
1 cup shredded Cheddar cheese
1 cup condensed cream of mushroom soup
3 cups packaged bread dressing prepared
    according to package instructions
¼ cup butter, melted

PREPARATION:

Step 1: Place chicken breasts in greased casserole and sprinkle with salt and pepper. Add sauteed mushrooms, cheese and soup. Sprinkle with dressing and drizzle butter over top.

Step 2: Bake at 350° 30 minutes, covered, then uncover and bake for 30 minutes more.

Makes 4 servings.

GOLD-FLECKED BROILED CHICKEN

INGREDIENTS:

1 large clove garlic, crushed
½ teaspoon salt
¼ teaspoon freshly ground black pepper
¼ teaspoon cayenne pepper
½ teaspoon fresh rosemary leaves, minced, or
    ¼ teaspoon dried rosemary leaves, crushed
Juice of 1 small lemon
1 tablespoon cornmeal
¼ cup oil
1 (3½-pound) chicken, cut up
Chopped parsley

PREPARATION:

Step 1: Mash garlic and salt together in small bowl with back of spoon. Mash in peppers and rosemary. Add lemon juice and cornmeal. Continue to mash until fairly smooth. Stir in oil.

Step 2: Place chicken in shallow dish. Pour cornmeal mixture over chicken, coating pieces well. Let stand 1 hour.

Step 3: Preheat broiling unit. Place chicken on broiling rack 5 inches from heat source. Broil 20 minutes on each side. Chicken is done when juices run yellow when pierced with fork. Garnish with parsley.

Makes 4 servings.

CHICKEN LOUISETTE

INGREDIENTS:

6-7 tablespoons unsalted butter
2 (2½-pound) chickens, cut for frying
1 small onion, thinly sliced
Salt
Freshly ground black pepper
¼ pound mushrooms, thinly sliced
1 package golden bouillon powder
3 tablespoons flour
½ cup dry white wine
1 cup chicken stock
¼ cup cooked ham, chopped
4 slices white bread, crusts removed
Chopped fresh parsley

PREPARATION:

Step 1: Melt 4 tablespoons butter in Dutch oven and brown chicken pieces slowly. Place onion on top of chicken. Season to taste with salt and pepper. Cover and cook slowly 30-40 minutes or until tender.

Step 2: Remove chicken. Add 2 more tablespoons of butter to pan and saute mushrooms until lightly browned, about 5 minutes.

Step 3: Turn off heat, blend in bouillon powder and flour. Pour in wine and stock and heat, stirring, until mixture comes to boil. Add ham to sauce and simmer 5 minutes. Return chicken to simmer 10 more minutes or until heated through.

Step 4: Cut slices of trimmed bread into triangles and saute in 1-2 tablespoons butter until golden brown. Arrange chicken on hot serving dish. Spoon on sauce. Arrange bread around chicken and sprinkle with parsley.

Makes 4 servings.

A DIFFERENT FRIED CHICKEN
(Advance Preparation Required)

INGREDIENTS:

12-20 chicken drumsticks or other
    chicken parts
Juice of 1 large lemon
⅓ cup soy sauce

Dash of salt
Dash of black pepper
½ cup flour
1½ cups oil

PREPARATION:
Step 1: Place drumsticks in deep rectangular casserole and sprinkle evenly with lemon juice. Pour soy sauce over chicken. Liquid should settle at bottom of casserole. Marinate overnight, making sure all sides of chicken are well marinated.
Step 2: Combine salt, pepper and flour in paper bag and drop drumsticks in, 1 at a time, shaking each time until well coated.
Step 3: Heat oil in deep skillet or fryer and fry chicken until golden.

GRILLED DRUMSTICKS
WITH APRICOT-DIJON JAM

INGREDIENTS:
¾ cup tomato juice
1 teaspoon paprika
1 teaspoon onion powder
1 teaspoon lemon-pepper seasoning
1 teaspoon salt
½ teaspoon garlic powder
⅛ teaspoon cayenne pepper
12 chicken drumsticks
½ cup apricot preserves
1-2 tablespoons Dijon mustard
1 tablespoon lemon juice

PREPARATION:
Step 1: Combine tomato juice, paprika, onion powder, lemon-pepper seasoning, salt, garlic powder and cayenne in shallow dish. Add drumsticks, cover and refrigerate 6 hours or overnight, turning occasionally.
Step 2: Grill chicken over low coals 45-60 minutes, turning frequently and brushing with remaining marinade.
Step 3· Meanwhile, combine preserves, mustard and lemon juice in small saucepan. Heat on outer edge of grill as chicken cooks. Serve as dip or sauce for chicken.

Makes 4-6 servings.

CHICKEN AND SAUSAGE GUMBO

INGREDIENTS:

2 whole chicken breasts, skinned and boned
3 tablespoons vegetable oil
8 ounces fully cooked smoked sausage,
    cut into ½-inch thick slices
3 tablespoons all-purpose flour
1 medium onion, chopped
1 small green bell pepper, seeded and chopped
½ cup chopped celery
1 garlic clove, minced
½ teaspoon salt
¼ teaspoon ground red pepper
1 can (16-ounce) stewed tomatoes, crushed
1 can (13-¾ ounce) chicken broth
8 ounces okra, cut into ½-inch thick slices, or 1
    package (10-ounce) frozen cut okra
3 cups cooked rice
Parsley for garnish (optional)

PREPARATION:

Step 1: Cut chicken into 1-inch cubes. In large sauce pot, heat oil over medium-high heat. Add chicken and sausage, a few pieces at a time, and cook until browned on all sides, removing to plate as they brown.

Step 2: Pour off drippings from sauce pot into a cup and add enough oil to measure 3 tablespoons. Return oil to sauce pot. Add flour and cook, stirring constantly, until mixture is dark brown, about 2 minutes.

Step 3: Remove sauce pot from heat. Add onion, green pepper, celery, garlic, salt, and red and black peppers, stirring until all the vegetables are crisp-tender.

Step 4: Return sauce pot to heat. Gradually stir in the tomatoes and chicken broth, then add the chicken and sausages.

Step 5: Bring mixture to a boil. Reduce heat, then cover and simmer until the chicken is tender, about 15 minutes.

Step 6: Add okra, then continue to simmer, covered, for 5 more minutes.

Step 7: To serve, spoon ½ cup cooked rice into each of 6 serving bowls. Spoon gumbo over rice. Top with parsley.

Serves 6.

HOT AND SOUR TURKEY WINGS

INGREDIENTS:

                4 turkey wings, about 4 pounds
                2 tablespoons oil
                1 (20-ounce) can pineapple chunks
                ¼ cup soy sauce
                2 tablespoons vinegar
                1 tablespoon sugar
                1 clove garlic, pressed
                2 teaspoons crushed dried red pepper flakes
                ½ teaspoon ground ginger
                1 cup green onion fans
                1 cup sweet red or green pepper strips
                1 tablespoon toasted sesame seeds

PREPARATION:

Step 1: Cut each wing into 2 pieces at joints, leaving tip with blade. Heat oil in large wok or Dutch oven. Brown wings slowly on all sides. Drain excess fat.

Step 2: Combine ⅓ cup syrup or juice from pineapple with soy sauce, vinegar, sugar, garlic, red pepper flakes and ginger. Pour over turkey wings. Cover and simmer 20 minutes or until tender.

Step 3: Add pineapple chunks, green onion fans and pepper strips. Simmer 10 minutes.

Step 4: Serve hot, sprinkled with toasted sesame seeds.

Makes 4-6 servings.

Note: To make green onion fans, cut 1½-inch lengths of green onion. Cut both ends in several lengthwise cuts. Place in ice water so ends will curl.

NICARAGUAN TURKEY

(Advance Preparation Required)

INGREDIENTS:

    1 turkey (12 pounds)
    3 cans beer
    3 tablespoons margarine
    3 tablespoons mustard
        (prepared — Dijon preferred)
    2 pound can whole tomatoes
    1 large onion
    4-5 pieces garlic
    1½ teaspoons Ortega chiles
    ¾ teaspoon thyme
    1 cup hot catsup
    ½ cup Worcestershire sauce
    3¼ ounces capers
    1 can pitted olives
    ½ cup raisins
    ½ cup pitted prunes
    1 cup dry sherry
    Salt to taste

PREPARATION:

Step 1: Pierce and marinate turkey overnight in beer, turning once.

Step 2: Discard beer and pat turkey dry. Rub inside and out with mustard and margarine mixed together.

Step 3: Place turkey, breast down, in roasting pan.

Step 4: Mix next seven ingredients and chop coarsely in a food processor or blender. Pour over turkey, cover and bake at 350° for 1 hour.

Step 5: Remove turkey from oven and turn breast side up.

Step 6: Add wine, capers, raisins, prunes and salt to pot and bake, covered, 30 minutes at 325°.

Step 7: Uncover turkey and bake 30 minutes more, or until done.

Step 8: Cool turkey, remove bones and skin, and skim fat from sauce.

Step 9: Arrange meat in baking dish and alternate with sauce. Heat and serve.

Serves 15-20 people.

ENTREES
(PORK)

In these days of awareness of cholesterol problems pork is rather frowned on, but man cannot live by oat bran alone so splurge a little.

ROAST PORK LOIN

INGREDIENTS:

4-4½ pound bone-in pork loin
1 tablespoon salt
1 teaspoon paprika
½ teaspoon caraway seeds, slightly crushed
2 cloves garlic, mashed
1 cup thinly sliced onion
½ cup thinly sliced carrots
2 cloves garlic, whole
6-8 crushed peppercorns
2 bay leaves
½ teaspoon marjoram
2-3 cups water
8 ounces ham hock or about 1
    pound pig's feet, optional

PREPARATION:

Step 1: Trim fat from pork loin, leaving just enough so as not to bare flesh. Mince trimmings very fine. Set aside.

Step 2: Rub entire surface of meat with salt. Let stand at room temperature for about 30 minutes while you prepare other ingredients.

Step 3: Sprinkle paprika and caraway seeds over surface of meat. With small, pointed knife, make holes no deeper than ¼ inch all over surface. Rub in garlic pulp and be sure some of pulp and, here and there a caraway seed, gets into crevices.

Step 4: Spread half onion and all the carrots, garlic cloves and peppercorns on bottom of roasting pan with tight-fitting lid. Place roast on top of vegetables.

Step 5: In small skillet over medium heat, cook remaining onion and small bits of fat until smoking hot and browned. Pour them evenly over meat. Crumble bay leaves and marjoram and sprinkle over meat. Pour about 2 cups of water in pan (3 if you have a pan with a large bottom surface). Roast meat uncovered about 30 minutes at 400°.

Step 6: Tilt pan and baste meat with drippings. Then cover, reduce heat to 325° and roast 1 hour, basting every 20 minutes. If liquid disappears from bottom of pan, add another cup of water — but never pour water on roast, always around it.

Step 7: To finish, remove cover, increase heat to 400° and roast 30 minutes, basting every 10 minutes. The internal temperature at thickest part of roast should register 150-155 degrees. Then remove roast and place it on carving board or large platter.

Step 8: Place strainer over bowl and pour pan juices (there won't be a lot, but deep brown and aromatic) through strainer. Press juce and as much of pulp of vegetables as possible through strainer. Discard whole spices and vegetable fibers.

Step 9: Adjust seasonings. You may have to dilute gravy a bit or reduce it by rapidly boiling in small pan without cover. There should not be more than about 2 tablespoons per serving.

Step 10: Slice roast and serve with gravy.

Makes 8 servings with leftovers for sandwiches.

HAWAIIAN PORK STEW

INGREDIENTS:
>2 pounds boneless pork shoulder
>¼ cup flour
>1 teaspoon ground ginger
>2 tablespoons oil
>1 (8-ounce) can pineapple chunks in juice
>⅓ cup bottled teriyaki sauce
>1 pound sweet potatoes, peeled
>1 large onion, cut into eighths

PREPARATION:
Step 1: Cut pork into 1½-inch cubes. Combine flour and ginger and use to coat pork. Reserve 2 tablespoons flour mixture.

Step 2: Brown pork on all sides in hot oil in Dutch oven.
Step 3: Drain pineapple and reserve juice. Add reserved juice, teriyaki sauce and 1 cup water to pork. Bring to boil, then reduce heat and simmer, covered, 1 hour, stirring occasionally.
Step 4: Cut sweet potatoes into 2-inch chunks. Add to pork and simmer, covered, 10 minutes. Stir in onion and simmer, covered, 20 minutes longer or until pork and yams are tender.
Step 5: Meanwhile, combine reserved flour mixture and ¾ cup water. Stir into pork mixture and cook until slightly thickened. Stir in pineapple and heat through.
Makes 6 servings.

MAPLE BAKED PORK CHOPS AND PEARS

INGREDIENTS:

>   6 loin pork chops, cut ¾-inch thick
>   1 teaspoon salt
>   ¼ teaspoon sage
>   2 pears
>   2 tablespoons cornstarch
>   1½ cups hot water
>   ½ cup maple syrup
>   2 tablespoons cider vinegar
>   Parsley

PREPARATION:
Step 1: Rub pork chops with ¼ teaspoon salt and sage. Brown slowly in hot skillet. Place in shallow baking dish. Core and slice pears, but do not peel. Arrange slices on top of pork chops.
Step 2: Blend cornstarch into fat drippings in skillet. Gradually stir in hot water and cook until thickened. Add syrup, vinegar and remaining ¾ teaspoon salt. Pour sauce over pork shops and pears.
Step 3: Cover and bake at 350 degrees about 1 hour or until pork chops are tender. Garnish with parsley.
Makes 6 servings.

ITALIAN SAUSAGE WITH GREEN PEPPERS AND ONIONS

INGREDIENTS:

3 pounds mild Italian sausage
¼ cup olive oil
2 medium onions, sliced
3 green peppers, peeled, seeded and
   cut into ¼-inch strips
1 tablespoon oregano
1 teaspoon basil
2 cloves garlic, chopped
2 cups canned, crushed and peeled
   Italian tomatoes
½ cup dry sherry
⅓ cup heavy (whipping) cream, optional

PREPARATION:

Step 1: Place sausage in large skillet with ½-inch water in bottom. Cook over medium heat until water evaporates. Add olive oil and saute a few minutes until browned on all sides.

Step 2: Remove sausage and add onions and green peppers. Season with oregano and basil. Saute until onions are golden brown. Add garlic and cook 1 minute longer. Add tomatoes. Simmer 5 minutes.

Step 3: Add sherry and cook over high heat until sherry is absorbed. Add sausages to sauce during last 2 minutes. Add cream, mixing well.

Makes 6-8 servings.

BEERY SAUSAGES AND SAUERKRAUT
(Advance Preparation Required)

INGREDIENTS:

1 (1-pound) package Polish sausages
1 (12-ounce) package bratwurst
1 (12-ounce) package veal knackwurst
1 tablespoon minced garlic
2 onions, thinly sliced
4 (11- to 12-ounce) cans or bottles of beer
1 small red pepper, roasted, peeled and seeded
1 small green pepper, roasted, peeled
   and seeded

1 (2-pound) jar sauerkraut, drained
    and very well rinsed
1 tablespoon butter or margarine
1 tablespoon oil
¾ cup apple juice

PREPARATION:
Step 1: Place sausages in single layer in 17×9-inch glass casserole. Sprinkle with garlic and arrange onions over top. Pour beer over all, cover with foil or plastic wrap and refrigerate 8 hours or overnight.
Step 2: About 1 hour before serving, cut red and green peppers into thin strips. Drain sausage mixture, discarding marinade, and grill onions and sausages until sausages are lightly browned.
Step 3: Lightly saute sauerkraut in butter and oil in large skillet. Place sausages and onions over sauerkraut and add apple juice. Cover and simmer until sausages are very tender and liquid is reduced by about half. Stir in peppers and cook 10 minutes longer.

Makes about 8 servings.

MEXICAN LASAGNA

INGREDIENTS:
½ pound jack cheese, shredded
1 pound breakfast sausage
3 cups Salsa Mexicana
1 (7-ounce) package corn tortillas
½ cup sour cream
¼ cup cilantro leaves

PREPARATION:
Step 1: Place sausage in skillet and cook over low heat until sausage is browned. Strain to remove fat. Chop sausage to fine consistency by hand or in food processor fitted with metal blade with 1-second pulses. Add sausage to Salsa Mexicana.
Step 2: Place 2 tortillas in bottom of 11×7-inch glass baking dish. Spread ¾ cup Salsa and ½ loosely packed shredded cheese over tortillas. Top with 2 more tortillas and continue layering, finishing with cheese.
Step 3: Adjust oven rack to lowest position. Bake at 350° 25 to 30 minues. Cool 15 minutes.
Step 4: Garnish with sour cream and cilantro leaves before serving.

Makes 6-8 servings.

SALSA MEXICANA
INGREDIENTS:

>2 medium cloves garlic, peeled
>1 large banana pepper (pale green), roasted, peeled, and seeded
>2 small onions, peeled and cubed
>2 tablespoons oil
>1 (28-ounce) can Italian plum tomatoes, drained
>1⅔ cups chicken or beef broth
>2 tablespoons chili powder
>1 teaspoon dried leaf oregano
>½ teaspoon ground cumin
>⅛ teaspoon salt
>¼ teaspoon black pepper
>¼ teaspoon cayenne pepper

PREPARATION:

Step 1: Mince garlic and finely chop peppers and onions. (Or fit food processor with metal blade. With machine running, drop garlic through food chute and process until minced. Add pepper and onions and chop with 1-second pulses.) Transfer to deep 10-inch skillet.

Step 2: Add oil. Cook over low heat until tender, about 5 minutes. Puree tomatoes by processing continually in processor or blender. Add to skillet. Add broth, chili powder, oregano, cumin, salt, pepper and cayenne pepper. Simmer 30 minutes, stirring occasionally.

Step 3: Cool to room temperature. Puree sauce in 2-cup batches before using.

BRONZE BAKED HAM

INGREDIENTS:

>1 (10- to 12-pound) boneless smoked ham
>Whole cloves
>2-3 cloves garlic, mashed
>1 tablespoon Dijon mustard
>½ cup chili sauce
>¾ cup brown sugar, packed
>1 tablespoon dark rum

PREPARATION:

Step 1: Line large roasting pan with foil. With sharp knife, score top of ham. Stud with cloves at every score.

Step 2: Combine garlic, mustard, chili sauce, brown sugar, and rum in small bowl. Mix well. Spread evenly over top and sides of ham.

Step 3: Bake at 400° for 1½ hours. Serve hot or cold.
Makes about 15 servings.

BEST HAM LOAF

INGREDIENTS:

        1½ pounds ground ham
        ½ pound ground pork
        2 eggs, slightly beaten
        ½ cup milk
        1 cup soft bread crumbs
        1 teaspoon dry mustard
        2 tablespoons chopped onion
        ⅛ teaspoon black pepper

PREPARATION:
Step 1: Combine ham, pork, eggs, milk, bread crumbs, mustard, onion and pepper. Mix well.
Step 2: Press lightly into greased 9×5-inch loaf pan and bake at 350° for 1 hour. Slice for serving.
Makes 1 (2-pound) loaf.

ORANGE-GLAZED HAM LOAF

INGREDIENTS:

        ½ cup orange juice
        1 tablespoon lemon juice
        1½ cups soft bread crumbs
        1 pound ground ham
        1 pound ground pork
        ¼ cup chopped onion
        2 tablespoons chopped parsley
        2 eggs, lightly beaten
        ¼ cup brown sugar, packed
        ½ teaspoon dry mustard
        1 teaspoon flour
        5 thin unpeeled orange slices

PREPARATION:

Step 1: Mix orange and lemon juices and pour over bread crumbs in mixing bowl. Add ham, pork, onion, parsley and eggs. Mix gently but thoroughly. Mix brown sugar, mustard and flour and sprinkle evenly in bottom of greased 9×5-inch loaf pan. Overlap orange slices on sugar mixture. Pack meat over oranges. Bake at 350° 1¼ hours. Turn out on platter.

Serves 8.

HAM CROQUETTES
WITH MUSTARD SAUCE

INGREDIENTS:

Croquette Sauce
2 cups finely diced or chopped ham
¼ cup finely chopped green pepper
1 teaspoon finely chopped onion
1 cup coarse soft bread crumbs
1 egg, beaten
¼ cup butter or chicken fat
Mustard Sauce

PREPARATION:

Step 1: Combine cooled Croquette Sauce with the ham, green pepper and onion; mix well. Chill for 30 minutes. Shape mixture into 6 patties. Roll in bread crumbs, then in beaten egg and again in crumbs.

Step 2: Saute coquettes in butter for about 10 minutes or until lightly browned. Serve with Mustard Sauce.

Yield: 6 portions.

CROQUETTE SAUCE

INGREDIENTS:

3 tablespoons butter or margarine
5 tablespoons flour
1 cup milk
¼ teaspoon salt
⅛ teaspoon pepper
1 teaspoon finely minced onion

½ teaspoon Worcestershire sauce
¼ teaspoon lemon juice

PREPARATION:

Step 1: Melt butter. Blend in flour to make a smooth paste. Add milk gradually, stirring until smooth. Add remaining ingredients.

Step 2: Cook over low heat, stirring constantly, until sauce is very thick. Cool thoroughly.

MUSTARD SAUCE

INGREDIENTS:

1 tablespoon butter or margarine
1 tablespoon flour
1 cup milk
3 tablespoons mayonnaise
2 tablespoons prepared mustard
1 tablespoon lemon juice
¼ teaspoon salt
Dash of pepper

PREPARATION:

Step 1: Melt butter. Blend in flour to make a smooth paste. Add milk gradually, stirring until smooth. Cook, stirring constantly, until sauce thickens slightly.

Step 2: Stir in mayonnaise, mustard and lemon juice. Cook over low heat until thickened. Add salt and pepper; mix well.

Step 3: Serve hot. Yield: 1 cup.

Note: This sauce keeps well in refrigerator. Always reheat over hot water.

FETTUCCINE WITH PEAS AND HAM

INGREDIENTS:

> 5 tablespoons unsalted butter
> ¼ pound shallots, minced
> ½ pound sliced mushrooms
> 1¼ cups heavy (whipping) cream
> 1 (10-ounce) package frozen tiny peas, thawed
> ¼ pound boiled ham, chopped
> 1 pound fettuccine, cooked al dente and drained
> Freshly grated Parmesan cheese
> Salt, freshly ground black pepper

PREPARATION:

Step 1: Melt butter in heavy large non-aluminum skillet. Add shallots and saute until soft. Add mushrooms, increase heat to high, and cook until mushrooms are very lightly browned.

Step 2: Add cream and let boil 2 minutes. Stir in peas and cook about 30 seconds. Reduce heat to low and blend in ham, fettuccine and 1 cup Parmesan cheese. Toss until heated, well-combined, and sauce clings to pasta.

Step 3: Season to taste with salt and pepper. Turn onto heated platter and serve with additional Parmesan cheese.

Makes 8 servings.

Note: Sauce may be prepared an hour or so ahead to point of adding peas.

ENTREES
(LAMB)

Some people find lamb to be too "pungent" a meat, but it is one of my favorites. Throughout Europe and the Middle East it is as popular as our beef is in America. Here we have a tendency to over-cook our lamb (it should always have a touch of **pink** to it) and the delicate flavor is lost.

I will give you a few recipes that I hope will convert you to the goodness of this wonderful meat. I prefer the lamb raised in the United States compared to that which is imported from New Zealand or Australia. Just don't let Crocodile Dundee know I said that!

MARINATED BUTTERFLY LAMB
(Advance Preparation Required)

INGREDIENTS:

> 1 (4 to 5 pound) leg of lamb, boned and butterflied.
> (your butcher will usually do this for you)
> 1 tsp. each oregano, thyme, rosemary, mint
> and cumin
> 4 or 5 cloves garlic, slivered
> 3 Tbsps. olive oil
> ¼ cup red wine vinegar
> Salt and freshly ground pepper
> ½ cup sherry

PREPARATION:

Step 1: Make several incisions on surface of lamb and insert slivers of garlic (use tip of knife to push through).

Step 2: Rub salt and pepper over all surfaces of meat.

Step 3: Combine oil, vinegar, sherry and herbs. Whisk together, and rub some of the mixture on meat surface.

Step 4: Put meat in glass baking pan and pour remaining marinade over meat.

Step 5: Put meat in refrigerator, cover with foil and let marinate 48 hours. Turn meat every 12 hours.

Step 6: Prepare barbecue grill with medium hot coals. Place meat (fat side down) on grill, and barbecue as you would a thick steak. Turn meat every few minutes and brush with remaining marinade.

Step 7: When meat is done (25-30 minutes) remove to cutting board and slice against the grain in thin slices.

Note: Remove meat from refrigerator at least an hour before cooking.

LAMB CHOPS CASSEROLE

INGREDIENTS:

> 4 loin lamb chops (1½ inches thick)
> 1 clove garlic
> Seasoned flour
> 8 tiny white onions
> 2 medium-carrots (cut in small matchlike strips)
> 1½ ozs. butter (3 Tbsp.)
> 1½ cups dry red wine
> 1 tsp. dried marjoram
> 4 large mushroom caps

PREPARATION:

Step 1:   Parboil the whole tiny white onions in salted water for 10 minutes. Drain and set aside. When cool enough, slip off the skins.

Step 2:   Rub lamb chops on both sides with clove of garlic and dust with seasoned flour.

Step 3:   Heat the butter in a heavy skillet. Add the parboiled onions, the sliced carrots, and the lamb chops. When the chops are lightly browned on both sides, transfer them and the browned vegetables to a heavy casserole.

Step 5:   Pour in the dry red wine and sprinkle with the dried marjoram. Cover the casserole tightly and place in a 325° oven and cook for 1 to 1½ hours, or until the chops are tender.

Step 5:   Saute large mushroom caps in butter for about 8 mins.

Step 6:   Transfer the chops and vegetables to a hot platter, top each chop with a large mushroom cap and pour the gravy over all.

Hashed brown potatoes and stewed tomatoes are an excellent accompaniment. Serve the same type of wine that was used in cooking the chops.

SOUTHERN OVEN-ROAST
LEG OF LAMB

INGREDIENTS:

  1 (5-6 lb) leg of lamb
  4 cloves garlic, slivered
  1½ cups cider vinegar
  ½ cup (packed) dark brown sugar
  7 or 8 pods dried red pepper
  Salt and freshly ground black pepper

PREPARATION:

Step 1: Wipe roast with damp clean towel. Make several incisions on surface of lamb and insert garlic slivers.

Step 2: In small saucepan bring vinegar and brown sugar to a boil. Lower heat to simmer and add red pepper pods. Simmer over low heat 15 mins.

Step 3: Heat oven to 325°

Step 4: Place lamb on rack in foil lined baking pan. Add a little water to pan and roast meat 30 mins. per pound, basting every seven minutes with vinegar mixture. Halfway through roasting time turn lamb over and baste in the same way. Add a bit more water to the pan to keep marinade from burning in bottom of pan. During the last ½ hour of cooking time use caramelized juices in pan for basting.

Step 5: Remove pan from oven and let roast stand for 10 minutes. Slice thinly and spoon a little of the pan juices over meat.

ENTREES
(VEAL)

Good veal is so expensive these days I'm giving you only one recipe...but it is terrific! The veal must be white, but the cut is less expensive than other cuts, and I promise you a real lip-smacker!

I found this recipe when I was in Luxembourg several years ago. There isn't a more gracious country in Europe (or, I should say "Duchy") so it's no wonder that this stew is practically their national dish...it's as wonderful as the country and the people who live there.

LUXEMBOURG VEAL STEW

INGREDIENTS:

> 2 lbs. veal shoulder
> Flour
> 3 Tbsps. butter
> 1 large onion, sliced
> 3 tomatoes, peeled and seeded
> 1 bay leaf
> 5 whole cloves
> Pinch each of thyme and marjoram
> Dash of cayenne
> 2½ cups light beer
> 5 gingersnaps
> Juice of half a lemon

PREPARATION:

Step 1: Cut veal into 1-inch cubes, roll them in flour and saute lightly in butter. Remove from pan and put aside for a moment.

Step 2: Saute sliced onion in same butter until golden.

Step 3: Put the meat and onion in a stewpan, add tomatoes (quartered) and all the seasonings. Add salt and pepper to taste.

Step 4: Add light beer, cover the pan tightly, and cook very slowly for 1½ hours.

Step 5: Moisten gingersnaps (I add two more than the recipe calls for) with water, crush into paste and add to the contents of the pan. Put the lid back on and continue cooking slowly for 30 minutes more.

STEP 6: Just before serving add the lemon juice. Serve with mashed potatoes.

PASTA DISHES

I can't resist throwing a few of my favorite pasta dishes into this book. After all, if they're good enough for Sophia Loren they can't be all bad. Miss Loren says she **diets** on pasta! Su-u-u-ure she does!

THREE CHEESE ZITI RING

INGREDIENTS:

½ pound ziti, cooked and drained
2 cups soft whole-wheat bread crumbs
1 cup shredded Cheddar cheese
1 cup shredded Swiss cheese
½ cup grated Parmesan cheese
¼ cup diced pimiento
2 tablespoons minced parsley
3 eggs, lightly beaten
1½ teaspoons salt
¼ teaspoon black pepper
½ cup minced green onions
1¾ cups milk
Mushroom Sauce

PREPARATION:
(Microwave)

Step 1: Combine ziti with bread crumbs, Cheddar, Swiss and Parmesan cheeses, pimiento, parsley, eggs, salt, and pepper in large bowl. Set aside.

Step 2: Place green onions and milk in 1-quart measure and microwave, uncovered, on HIGH (100% power) 4½-5½ minutes until small bubbles appear around edge. Stir into ziti-cheese mixture.

Step 3: Spoon into ungreased 2-quart ring mold, cover with vented plastic wrap and microwave on MEDIUM (50% power) 9-10 minutes, rotating mold 180 degrees after half the cooking time, just until firm. (The soft area midway between edge and center will set on standing.)

Step 4: Cover with foil and allow to stand 10 minutes. Invert on heated platter and gently ease cheese ring out of mold. Serve with Mushroom Sauce, prepared by microwave while ziti ring stands.

Makes 6-8 servings.

MUSHROOM SAUCE

INGREDIENTS:

2 cups coarsely chopped mushrooms
¼ cup butter or margarine
¼ cup flour
2 cups milk
½ teaspoon salt
Dash black pepper

PREPARATION:

Step 1: Microwave mushrooms in butter in 2-quart casserole, covered with paper towels, on HIGH (100% power) 3½-4 minutes until limp, stirring after half the cooking time.

Step 2: Mix in flour and microwave, uncovered on HIGH 30 seconds, until foamy. Mix in milk, salt and pepper and microwave, uncovered on HIGH, 4½-5½ minutes, stirring after 2½ minutes until sauce boils and thickens. Stir again before serving.

Makes 2½ cups.

PENNE RUSTICA

INGREDIENTS:

¼ cup extra-virgin olive oil
½ small onion, finely diced
4 ounces pancetta, coarsely chopped
6 ounces ricotta cheese
Grated imported Parmesan cheese
¼ cup chopped fresh Italian parsley
Salt, pepper
1 pound imported Italian rigatoni

PREPARATION:

Step 1: Heat oil in small skillet. Add onion and cook over low heat until softened. Add pancetta and cook over medium heat until fat is rendered, but not crisp. Remove from heat.

Step 2: Place onion-pancetta mixture, including fat, in small mixing bowl. Add ricotta, ¼ cup Parmesan cheese, parsley, and salt and pepper to taste. Mix thoroughly with wooden spoon.

Step 3: Meanwhile, cook pasta in boiling salted water until tender. Drain, reserving 2-3 tablespoons cooking water.

Step 4: Place ricotta-pancetta mixture in large serving bowl. Add 2 to 3 Tbsp. cooking water and mix well. Add rigatoni and toss to mix well. Serve at once with additional Parmesan cheese, if desired.

Makes 4-6 servings.

RED PEPPER AND MOSTACCIOLI

INGREDIENTS:

2 tablespoons olive oil
3 cloves garlic, minced
1 stalk celery, minced
½ onion, minced
1 large sweet red pepper, minced
2 (1-pound) cans Italian plum tomatoes
10 black olives, pitted and sliced
10 stuffed green olives, sliced
1 teaspoon crushed or ground oregano
1 teaspoon crushed basil
½ teaspoon garlic salt
1 teaspoon capers
1 teaspoon crushed dried chiles
Salt, pepper
1 (12-ounce) package mostaccioli
2 tablespoons butter
Grated Parmesan cheese

PREPARATION:

Step 1: Heat olive oil in skillet and saute garlic, celery, onion, and minced red pepper until tender. Place undrained tomatoes in food processor or blender and chop slightly. Do not puree.

Step 2: Add tomatoes to skillet and simmer 10 minutes. Stir in black and green olives, oregano, basil, garlic salt, capers and chiles. Simmer, uncovered 20 minutes longer or until of desired consistency. Season to taste with salt and pepper.

Step 3: Cook mostaccioli according to package directions, drain well and toss with butter. Toss noodles with sauce. Serve cheese and, if desired, additional dried chiles at table.

Makes about 6 servings.

PASTA WITH GARLIC SAUCE

INGREDIENTS:

    1 pound thin spaghetti or vermicelli
    4 cloves garlic, crushed
    ¼ teaspoon crushed red pepper flakes
    3 tablespoons green olive oil
    ½ cup chopped fresh Italian parsley
    ½ cup freshly grated Parmesan cheese

PREPARATION:

Step 1: Cook pasta according to package directions just to al dente stage. In a large skillet, saute garlic and hot chile flakes in oil 2-3 minutes. Drain pasta well and add to skillet.

Step 2: Toss with oil; add parsley and cheese, mixing well. Heat for 1 minute. Serve immediately.

Makes 6 servings.

PASTA SHELLS WITH ZUCCHINI

INGREDIENTS:

    2 tablespoons butter or margarine
    1 clove garlic, minced
    3 or 4 zucchini, sliced
    1 teaspoon fresh rosemary leaves
    Salt, pepper
    1 pound large pasta shells
    2 quarts boiling salted water
    2 tablespoons chopped fresh marjoram
        or parsley
    ⅓ cup grated Parmesan cheese

PREPARATION:

Step 1: Melt butter over medium heat in large skillet. Add garlic and zucchini and cook until tender-crisp. Add rosemary and season to taste with salt and pepper. Turn up heat and cook 1-2 minutes to blend flavors. Remove from heat and set aside.

Step 2: Cook pasta shells in boiling salted water. Drain and turn into zucchini mixture. Place pan over low heat and toss to coat shells with sauce. Sprinkle with marjoram and cheese and toss again.

Makes 6-8 servings.

NOODLES WITH SESAME SAUCE

INGREDIENTS:

2 small green onions, ends trimmed,
    rinsed and patted dry
4 quarts water
½ pound fresh thin Chinese noodles
    (lo mein), linguine or spaghetti
1 small clove garlic, peeled
½ cup sesame paste (Oriental or Middle Eastern)
    or plain peanut butter
2 tablespoons shaoshing wine or dry sherry
2 tablespoons sesame oil
1 teaspoon dark soy sauce
1 teaspoon light soy sauce
½ teaspoon red chili oil
½ teaspoon white vinegar
¼ teaspoon sugar
3-5 tablespoons chicken broth

PREPARATION:

Step 1: Insert medium (4-millimeter) slicing disc in food processor container. With machine running, dangle-slice about 1 inch of white part of green onions by lowering through food chute. Turn over onions and make green onion slices by carefully lowering part of green top through food chute while machine is running. Do not allow fingers to enter chute. Reserve remaining onion for another use. Set green slices aside for garnish. Return processor container to base without washing.

Step 2: Heat 4 quarts water to boiling. Add noodles and boil until tender. Drain well and rinse with cold water to stop cooking and to remove starch. Set noodles aside until serving time. If noodles stick together, rinse in cool water and drain well before serving.

Step 3: Insert metal blade in processor container. With machine running, drop garlic through food chute and process until minced. Add sesame paste, wine, sesame oil, dark and light soy sauces, chili oil, vinegar and sugar. Process until thoroughly mixed.

Step 4: Add 3 tablespoons chicken broth and process until thick. Add additional chicken broth, if necessary. Transfer to bowl or jar and cover until ready to use, up to several hours.

Step 5: At serving time, divide noodles into separate portions in individual bowls, or place on serving platter. Top with sauce and garnish with green onions.

Makes 4-6 servings.

MACARONI AND CHEESE WITH CHILES

INGREDIENTS:

> 2 cups medium elbow macaroni
> ¼ cup butter
> 3 tablespoons flour
> 1 teaspoon salt
> ¼ teaspoon garlic powder
> ⅛ teaspoon black pepper
> 3 cups milk
> ¼ cup grated onion
> 1 (4-ounce) can diced green chiles
> 1 (2-ounce) jar pimiento, chopped
> 3 cups shredded Jack cheese
> ½ cup crushed tortilla chips
> Paprika

PREPARATION:

Step 1: Cook macaroni until tender but firm, then drain. Melt butter in large saucepan. Blend in flour, salt, garlic powder and pepper. Cook, stirring constantly, 2 minutes. Slowly add milk, stirring until smooth. Add onion, chiles and pimiento. Cook until thickened. Stir in cheese and cook until cheese is melted.

Step 2: Combine macaroni and cheese sauce. Pour into 2½-quart casserole. Top with crushed tortilla chips and sprinkle with paprika. Bake at 350° for 25 minutes. Serve immediately.

Makes 6-8 servings.

SOME "VEGGIES"
AND OTHER GOOD THINGS

Vegetables are good for you...we've been told since childhood that we would never grow up strong unless we ate our spinach and our broccoli. Now that we know steamed vegetables are best for us they are no longer boiled into grey tasteless matter, and that's certainly a plus. Most of these recipes are starches though, so you can always get your kids to eat that!

SCALLOPED POTATOES

INGREDIENTS:

> 4 large potatoes, thinly sliced
> 1 large onion, chopped
> ¼ cup milk
> 1 can cream of chicken soup
> ¼ cup sliced Cheddar cheese
> Grated Parmesan cheese
> Salt & pepper

PREPARATION:

Step 1: Combine potatoes and onions in 2-quart casserole dish.

Step 2: Blend soup and milk and pour over potatoes. Cover top with thin cheese slices. Sprinkle with Parmesan, salt and pepper, and ½ teaspoon paprika (optional). Bake at 350-370° for 1½ hours.

Serves 6.

BOB'S TEMPTATION

INGREDIENTS:

    1 large onion, thinly sliced
    4 tablespoons butter
    4 medium potatoes, thinly sliced
    3-4 anchovies (or pickled herring)
    ¾-1 cup milk

PREPARATION:

Step 1: Saute onion in 1 tablespoon butter until golden and sweet.

Step 2: Butter casserole (2-quart) with 1 tablespoon butter.

Step 3: Layer half the potatoes in casserole; top with onions; dot with pieces of chopped anchovies or herring. Cover with remaining potatoes; dot with remaining 2 tablespoons of butter.

Step 4: Bake at 400° for 10 minutes. Add ½ cup milk and bake for 10 minutes more. Add enough milk to barely cover. Continuing baking until done, about 30 more minutes.

Serves 6.

GARLIC POTATOES

INGREDIENTS:

    5 ounces small new potatoes, unpeeled, quartered lengthwise
    2 cloves garlic, halved
    ½ teaspoon salt
    Water
    1 tablespoon butter, softened
    2 teaspoons finely chopped green onion or chives

PREPARATION:

Step 1: Place potatoes, garlic and salt in small saucepan. Add water to cover and bring to boil. Cover pan loosely and cook 8-10 minutes or until tender. Drain, reserving potatoes and garlic.

Step 2: Remove garlic and crush with flat side of knife. Combine garlic with butter and green onion. Add to potatoes, tossing to coat. Serve immediately.

Serves 2.

HERB-BASTED POTATOES

INGREDIENTS:

6 Russet potatoes, cut in halves lengthwise
1 cup butter, melted
2 tablespoons paprika
1 tablespoon salt
1 tablespoon Italian seasoning
1 tablespoon garlic powder
1 tablespoon barbecue spice
White pepper
Lemon pepper

PREPARATION:

Step 1: Parboil potatoes just until tender. Melt butter in saucepan and add paprika, salt, Italian seasoning, garlic powder, and barbecue spice. Mix well.

Step 2: Place potatoes on baking sheet. Generously brush butter mixture over all sides of potato halves. Season to taste with white and lemon pepper. Bake at 350° 25-30 minutes.

Makes 6 servings.

POTATOES IN THE OVEN

INGREDIENTS:

1 (2-pound) package frozen hash browns, Southern style (thawed)
¼ cup plus 1 tablespoon butter or margarine
¼ cup chopped onion
¼ teaspoon white or black pepper
1 (8-ounce) package shredded Cheddar cheese
1 (8-ounce) carton sour cream
1 (10 ¾-ounce) can cream of chicken soup
½ cup cereal or cracker crumbs

PREPARATION:

Step 1: Place hash browns, ¼ cup margarine, onion, pepper, cheese, sour cream and soup in large greased baking dish. Mix until blended. Combine remaining 2 tablespoons margarine with cereal or cracker crumbs and sprinkle over top.

Step 2: Cover and bake at 350° for 40-50 minutes or until bubbly.

Makes about 6 servings.

EGGS, POTATOES AND CHEESE

INGREDIENTS:

4 eggs, separated
4 cups seasoned, hot mashed potatoes
2 cups shredded Swiss cheese
2 tablespoons finely chopped chives
2 tablespoons chopped green pepper
2 tablespoons chopped parsley
2 tablespoons diced pimiento
⅛ teaspoon black pepper
Dash paprika

PREPARATION:

Step 1: Beat egg whites until stiff peaks form. Beat yolks, 1 at a time, into hot mashed potatoes in another large bowl. Stir in cheese, chives, green pepper, parsley, pimiento and pepper. Fold in beaten egg whites and stir until thoroughly mixed.

Step 2: Spoon mixture into buttered 6-cup baking dish. Bake at 375° for 40 minutes, until puffed and golden. Sprinke with paprika and serve.

Makes 6 servings.

SWEET POTATO PONE

INGREDIENTS:

½ pound unsalted butter
¾ cup brown sugar, packed
8 eggs
4 cups grated sweet potatoes
1 cup orange juice
6 tablespoons molasses
2 tablespoons whiskey
Grated zest of 4 lemons
1½ teaspoons ground cinnamon
1 teaspoon ground nutmeg
1 teaspoon ground cloves
Salt, pepper

PREPARATION:

Step 1: Cream butter and sugar together in mixer bowl. Add eggs and beat. Beat in potatoes, orange juice, molasses, whiskey, lemon zest, cinnamon, nutmeg and cloves. Season to taste with salt and pepper.

Step 2: Turn into buttered 12×7-inch baking dish. Bake at 325° for 1 hour.
Makes 8 servings.

WHISKEY BEANS

INGREDIENTS:
> 2 (16-oz.) cans B.M. beans
> 1 tablespoon molasses
> ½ cup chili sauce
> 1 tablespoon dry mustard
> ½ cup strong coffee
> ½ pint bourbon
> ½ cup crushed pineapple
> ¼ cup brown sugar, packed

PREPARATION:
Step 1: Combine all ingredients except brown sugar and pineapple, and place in 2-quart casserole dish. Cover and let stand at room temperature for 4 hours.
Step 2: Place casserole in 350° oven for 45 minutes, covered. Uncover and top with pineapple and then brown sugar. Return to oven and bake for additional 35 minutes.
Serves 8-10.

COMPANY RICE

INGREDIENTS:
> ½ cup butter or margarine
> 1 large onion, minced
> ¾ cup shredded Cheddar cheese
> 1¾ cups uncooked rice
> 1 (4 ounce) can mushrooms, drained
> 2 (10½-ounce) cans consomme
> 1 cup sliced almonds

PREPARATION:
Step 1: Melt butter in skillet, add onion and saute until tender, but not browned. Combine onion, cheese, rice, mushrooms, consomme and almonds in 4-5 qt. casserole. Mix well.
Step 2: Cover and bake at 325° for 1 hour. Remove cover and bake 15 minutes longer.
Makes 10-12 servings.

REUBEN'S CREAMED CORN

INGREDIENTS:
>1½ cups half and half
>2 chicken bouillon cubes
>Dash white pepper
>2 teaspoons sugar
>2 (10-ounce) packages frozen cut corn, thawed
>2 tablespoons butter
>2 tablespoons flour
>Chopped parsley

PREPARATION:

Step 1: Blend together half and half, chicken bouillon cubes, pepper and sugar in saucepan. Bring to boil. Add corn to boiling liquid. Return to boil, reduce heat and simmer 3-5 minutes.

Step 2: Melt butter in separate small saucepan. Add flour and cook, stirring constantly, until paste is formed. Add flour mixture to corn mixture and stir with wooden spoon to mix well. Bring to boil, stirring frequently, until thickened.

Step 3: Remove from heat. Sprinkle lightly with chopped parsley.

Serves 6-8.

CORN PUDDING

INGREDIENTS:
>2 (15½-16 oz.) cans cream style corn
>1 cup milk
>½ cup butter, melted
>2 tablespoons sugar
>2 tablespoons flour
>2 beaten eggs
>Salt to taste

PREPARATION:

Step 1: Grease 2-quart casserole. Mix sugar and flour together in separate small cup.

Step 2: Blend all ingredients together, stirring in sugar-flour mixture, and place in casserole. Bake at 350° for 2 hours.

Serves 6-8.

GRITS WITH FRESH CORN AND TOMATOES

INGREDIENTS:

> 3 cups water
> ¾ cup grits
> 2 tablespoons butter
> 1 medium onion, chopped
> 2 cloves garlic, crushed and minced
> 1 small green pepper, diced
> 2 tablespoons canned chopped green chiles
> 1 pound Italian plum tomatoes,
>   peeled and chopped
> 2 cups cooked fresh corn kernels,
>   cut from 2-3 ears
> ½ teaspoon ground cumin
> ½ teaspoon dried oregano, crumbled
> Freshly ground pepper
> 1 cup shredded Cheddar cheese or
>   combination Cheddar and Jack cheeses

PREPARATION:

Step 1: Bring water to boil in heavy-bottomed saucepan. Slowly sprinkle in grits, stirring to avoid lumps. Lower heat immediately and cook over very low heat, stirring often, until thick and creamy, about 25 minutes.

Step 2: Meanwhile, melt butter in medium skillet. Saute onion and garlic until onion is translucent. Add green pepper and saute until tender. Add canned green chiles and tomatoes. Saute 5-7 minutes more until tender. Stir in corn, cumin, oregano and season to taste with pepper.

Step 3: When grits are cooked, stir into skillet. Sprinkle cheese over top, fold in and continue cooking until cheese melts.

Makes 4-6 servings.

Note: Regular or long-cooking grits taste of sweet creamed corn, while instant grits have virtually no flavor.

CORN CAKES

INGREDIENTS:

 1½ cups fresh or frozen corn kernels
 ½ cup milk
 ⅓ cup yellow cornmeal
 ⅓ cup flour
 ¼ cup butter, melted
 2 eggs
 2 egg yolks
 ½ teaspoon salt
 ¼ teaspoon black pepper
 2 tablespoons chopped chives
 Oil

PREPARATION:

Step 1: Roughly chop corn kernels or process in short bursts in food processor until chunky but creamy consistency is reached. Place in large bowl and whisk in milk, cornmeal and flour, making sure there are no lumps.

Step 2: In separate bowl, whisk together melted butter, whole eggs and egg yolks. Stir into corn mixture and add salt, pepper and chives.

Step 3: Heat oil in large saute pan over medium-high heat and spoon in batter to make pancakes size of silver dollars. Fry 2 minutes, or until golden brown on 1 side; then flip over and fry 2 more minutes. Remove from pan using slotted spatula. Place 4 cooked corn cakes on each serving plate.

Note: Serve with spicy vegetable or fruit relish. Makes about 2 dozen.

HOPPIN' JOHN
(Advanced Preparation Required)

INGREDIENTS:

 3 cups black-eyed peas
 Water or chicken broth
 3 pounds smoked ham hocks
 1 large onion, chopped
 1 bay leaf
 1 jalapeno pepper, minced
 Salt and pepper
 Dash cayenne pepper
 1 cup uncooked rice

Steamed collard greens
Chopped green onions

PREPARATION:

Step 1: Cover peas generously with water and soak overnight.

Step 2: Drain peas and place in kettle. Add ham hocks, onion, bay leaf, jalapeno, salt and pepper to taste, and cayenne pepper. Cover with water or broth and bring to boil. Cover kettle and simmer about 2½ hours.

Step 3: Remove ham hocks from kettle and cool slightly; remove skin and bones and excess fat from ham hocks and return meat to kettle. Remove and discard bay leaf.

Step 4: Bring 1½ cups water to boil in 2-quart saucepot. Add rice, cover and cook slowly over low flame until rice is tender, about 25-30 minutes.

Step 5: Serve hot ham and pea mixture over rice with steamed collard greens. Garnish with green onions. Makes 6 servings.

Note: Rice may be cooked in the same pot with the peas and ham hocks; the dish will taste even better but it won't look as pretty.

BROCCOLI PARMESAN

INGREDIENTS:

> 2 (10-ounce) packages frozen broccoli spears, thawed
> 4 eggs, beaten
> 1-2 cups grated Parmesan cheese
> 1-2 cups bread crumbs
> Oil for deep frying
> 1 quart homemade or bottled spaghetti sauce
> 8 ounces sliced mozzarella cheese

PREPARATION:

Step 1: Dip thawed broccoli spears in beaten eggs, then dip in Parmesan cheese and bread crumbs to coat evenly. Place in covered container and store in refrigerator overnight.

Step 2: Next day, heat oil in deep fryer and fry broccoli, a few at a time, until golden brown. Layer half of spaghetti sauce in 11×9-inch pan. Place single layer broccoli spears on top. Cover with remaining spaghetti sauce. Top with mozzarella cheese.

Step 3: Bake at 350° for 30 minutes.
Makes 6 servings.

AMBER ONIONS

INGREDIENTS:

> 9 medium white or yellow onions
> 1 teaspoon salt
> ¼ teaspoon paprika
> 2 tablespoons butter, melted
> ¼ cup tomato juice
> 3 tablespoons honey

PREPARATION:

Step 1: Cut onions in half laterally. Place in greased large shallow casserole.

Step 2: Combine salt, paprika, melted butter, tomato juice and honey. Pour over onions. Cover dish and bake at 300° for 1 hour or until onions are tender.

Makes about 9 servings.

PAPRIKA ONIONS

INGREDIENTS:

> 4 large onions, peeled and halved crosswise
> Boiling salted water
> ¼ cup oil
> 2 tablespoons vinegar
> 2 tablespoons honey
> ½ teaspoon salt
> ½ teaspoon dry mustard
> ½ teaspoon paprika
> ¼ teaspoon rubbed sage

PREPARATION:

Step 1: Place onions, cut sides up, in single layer in large skillet. Add enough boiling salted water to almost cover. Cover pan and cook gently 10 minutes. Drain.

Step 2: In saucepan, combine oil, vinegar, honey, salt, mustard, paprika and sage. Heat just to boiling and pour over onions. Cook, covered, over very low heat for 30 minutes or until tender. Baste occasionally to glaze.

Makes 4 servings.

FRIED BABY SPINACH LEAVES

INGREDIENTS:

> 1 bunch baby spinach
> 3 tablespoons peanut oil

PREPARATION:

> Wash spinach leaves, cut off stems and dry well. Heat oil
> to 375° and add leaves. Stir-fry until leaves are crisp and
> translucent, being careful to avoid splattering. Remove
> leaves to paper towels to drain. Salt lightly.

Serves 2.

BOMBAY PALACE NINE
VEGETABLE CURRY

INGREDIENTS:

> ¼ pound broccoli, cut into flowerets
> ¼ pound green or sweet red pepper, cut into
>   diamonds or small cubes
> ¼ pound carrots, peeled, sliced and cut into
>   diamonds or small cubes
> ¼ pound cauliflower, cut into flowerets
> ¼ pound green beans, sliced and cut into
>   diamonds or small cubes
> 1 large potato, peeled, sliced and cut into
>   diamonds or small cubes
> 2 tablespoons butter
> 1 large onion, minced
> 2 cloves garlic, minced
> 2 tomatoes, chopped
> 2 tablespoons yogurt
> Dry Masala
> ¼ cup water
> ½ cup heavy (whipping) cream
> ¼ pound fresh or ½ package frozen
>   green peas, thawed
> 1 (4-ounce) can fruit cocktail, drained
> ¼ cup raisins
> 12 slivered, blanched almonds

PREPARATION:

Step 1: Separately cook broccoli, green pepper, carrots, cauliflower, green beans and potato in boiling salted water until tender-crisp. Drain. Set aside.

Step 2: Melt butter in skillet. Add onion and garlic. Saute until onion is transparent.

Step 3: Add tomatoes, yogurt and Dry Masala to skillet. Simmer 5 minutes longer, adding ¼ cup water. Cover and simmer 10 minutes.

Step 4: Add heavy cream and peas. Remove a few cherry pieces from canned fruit for garnish. Add the remaining fruit to sauce.

Step 5: Just before serving, top with raisins and almonds and decorate with cherry pieces.

Makes 4-6 servings.

DRY MASALA

COMBINE:

> ½ teaspoon ground cardamom
> ½ teaspoon ground coriander
> ½ teaspoon ground ginger
> ½ teaspoon chili powder
> ½ teaspoon ground turmeric

TOMATO PUFF

INGREDIENTS:

> 2 slices bread, crusts removed
> ½ cup milk
> 2 tablespoons butter or margarine
> 5 tomatoes, peeled and chopped
> 1 teaspoon onion juice
> Salt, pepper
> 4 egg yolks, slightly beaten
> 5 egg whites, beaten stiff
> 2 tablespoons grated Parmesan cheese
> Paprika

PREPARATION:

Step 1: Soak bread in milk, then stir to paste consistency.

Step 2: Melt butter in skillet, add tomatoes, onion juice and salt and pepper to taste. Cook and stir until blended. Stir in bread paste. Remove from heat and stir in egg yolks. Cool.

Step 3: Fold yolk mixture into beaten whites and pour into a well-greased 2-quart souffle dish or casserole. Sprinkle with cheese and bake at 350° 35-40 minutes.

Step 4: Remove casserole from oven, sprinkle with paprika, and serve at once.

Makes 6 servings.

SIMPLE VEGETABLES WITH A LITTLE ZEST

One: **ITALIAN STIR FRIED BROCCOLI:**

Prepare 4 cups of broccoli flowerets (use only the top part of broccoli...save the stems, peel them and add them to soups, or thinly sliced they make a nice accompaniment when cooked with green peas.)

Heat 3 Tbsps. olive oil in large skillet. Add 4 cloves garlic (thickly sliced) to oil and fry until browned. Remove garlic and discard. Add 1 tsp. crushed red pepper flakes to hot oil and stir a few seconds. Now add broccoli and stir fry for two minutes. Pour three tablespoons water over all, cover tightly and lower heat. Cook for three minutes or until broccoli is crisp tender.

Two: **GLAZED CARROTS:**

Peel and slice diagonally enough carrots to make 4 cups. Put in sauce pan and add enough water just to cover. Add ¼ cup of dark rum, 1½ Tbsps. sugar and 3 Tbsps. butter. Bring to a boil over medium high heat and cook, uncovered, until most of liquid is evaporated and carrots are nicely glazed.

Three: **STRING BEANS:**

Snap ends off of beans and add to large sauce pan of boiling water. Boil exactly 8 minutes. Drain and rinse with cold water to stop cooking process. Place beans in refrigerator until ready to use (I do this early in the day). When ready to serve, heat 2 Tbsps. butter in saucepan and toss beans until moisture is gone. While beans are cooking (the first boiling process) add two slices of lean bacon (finely chopped) and 2 Tbsps. minced onion to small fry pan. Fry until lightly browned, drain and set aside.

Add the above mixture plus 1 tsp. of sugar and 1 tsp. of cider vinegar to reheatd beans, stir until hot and serve.

Four: PARSNIP AND POTATO PUREE:

Peel four medium-sized parsnips and core them. Boil in lightly salted water until quite tender, mash them and then add to 3 or 4 cups of mashed potatoes.

Whip mixture until blended and then add salt, pepper (white preferably) and butter to taste. Thin with a little heavy cream until a nice puree is achieved.

Five: BRUSSEL SPROUTS:

Rinse sprouts in cold water and peel off any thick or yellowed outer leaves. Place in saucepan filled with cold water, add sprouts and bring to boil. Now drain the sprouts and add to fresh pan of boiling, lightly salted water. Cook until just tender, drain, and cover with cold water to stop cooking process.

When sprouts are cool, slice in half the long way.

Blend together 1 Tbsp. seasoned rice vinegar, ½ tsp. of dry mustard, and ⅓ cup sourcream.

Toss sliced sprouts in saucepan with 1½ Tbsps. of butter until heated, add sour cream mixture and toss all **lightly** just until heated. Do not let **boil.**

DESSERTS

And now we come to the inevitable climax of any decent dinner.

It is a known fact that desserts are the devil's handiwork. If God had approved of desserts we would all have been born with our tiny fists wrapped around a baggie full of dentures. Yet **He** did invent the apple (the world's first known dessert)!

Forget the mess **that** temptation got us into, and get on with the "up" side of this segment. There has to be something good to say in favor of the dreaded sweetmeat.

Think of the millions of children who would never have eaten carrots, peas, broccoli and spinach without the most famous admonition of our childhood: "No vegetables, no dessert!"

Of course I'm speaking of **real** desserts. Not fluff-filled cupcakes packaged in ancient cellophane. Not those unmentionable snacks that have only one identifiable ingredient. . . sugar!

How often have we all labored through a soggy tuna-helper casserole knowing, in our heart of hearts, that somewhere in the refrigerator, tucked between the cottage cheese and the buttermilk, is some incredible confection calling out, "Here I am! All's right with the world!". (And I'm not talking about apricot leather or a stewed peach mired on a square of shimmering gelatin.)

If there is anything cautionary to be said against desserts, the warning goes to those unfortunates who suffer from diabetes; to the children who start running around in circles babbling a blue streak and setting fire to the bird-cage; or, worse yet, when that new computerized talking scale of yours mutters, in very disagreeable tones, "If your ears were just a tad bigger you'd have a good shot at winning the "Dumbo look-alike" contest".

Now let's get those salivary glands in motion and jump right into the preparation of my favorite cheesecake.

(Authors note: No book these days seems to be complete without a bit of name-dropping, so to satisfy this current fad I will tell you that this happens to be Burt Lancaster's favorite cheesecake, too!)

LEMON GLAZED CHEESECAKE

INGREDIENTS:

      1½ Tbsps. butter
      ½ cup graham cracker crumbs
      12 ounces softened cream cheese
      ¾ cup sugar
      4 egg yolks
      2 Tbsps. flour
      1½ tsps. vanilla
      1 tsp. finely grated lemon peel
      ½ tsp. salt
      2 cups scalded light cream (I use 1
        cup half and half and 1 cup whipping cream)
      4 egg whites

PREPARATION:

Step 1: Grease 8-inch springform pan with butter. Turn pan on its side and put in graham cracker crumbs. Keep turning pan so that crumbs stick to sides. Now let the rest of crumbs cover bottom of pan. Put springform pan in freezer for ½ hour.

Step 2: Preheat oven to slow (300°).

Step 3: Beat together softened cream cheese, sugar, egg yolks, flour, vanilla, lemon peel and salt until smooth. (I do this in my food processor.)

Step 4: Gradually pour in scalded cream.

Step 5: Beat egg whites until stiff but not dry.

Step 6: Transfer cream cheese mixture to large bowl, and fold egg whites into mixture, lightly but thoroughly.

Step 7: Remove pan from freezer and pour in mixture. Set pan in another shallow pan containing 1 inch of hot water and bake 1½ hours.

Step 8: Remove pan from oven and let cool on wire rack for 1 hour.

TO PREPARE GLAZE:

Step 1: In heavy one-quart saucepan mix ½ cup sugar, 1½ Tbsps. cornstarch, and ¼ tsp. salt.

Step 2: Combine ¾ cup water, ⅓ cup lemon juice, and 1 egg yolk. Add to sugar mixture.

Step 3: Cook over low heat, stirring constantly, until mixture comes to slow boil and is thickened.

Step 4: Add 1 Tbsp. sweet butter and 1 tsp. grated lemon rind.

Step 5: Remove from heat and let cool slightly (about 15 to 20 mins.) but spread on cheesecake before glaze sets.

Place springform pan in refrigerator and let chill for at least six hours. I make this cake the day before. and after a few hours cover it with foil.

Do not remove from springform pan until ready to serve.

NOTE: If you like, (instead of the lemon glaze), the cake can be covered with whole small strawberries and then glazed with a little melted currant jelly. Do this about an hour before serving.

For the chocoholic here are a couple of recipes that will probably make you feel as if you are dooming yourself to a fat farm in Purgatory, but I say "The hell with it!" Only one **little** piece can't be all that bad for you. (Ho-Ho-Ho)

CHOCOLATE DAMNATION

INGREDIENTS:
>
> ¾ pound semisweet chocolate pieces or squares
> ¼ cup strong coffee
> 2 eggs, separated
> ¼ cup coffee flavored liqueur
> 3 Tbsps. sugar
> ¼ cup whipping cream
> Brownie shell
> Chocolate Glaze

PREPARATION:
Step 1: Melt chocolate with coffee in top of double boiler. Remove from heat.
Step 2: Beat egg yolks until pale yellow in color and stir in some of the chocolate mixture. Return to chocolate in pan, stirring until smooth.
Step 3: Gradually stir in liqueur and cool.
Step 4: Beat egg whites until foamy. Gradually add sugar and beat until stiff.
Step 5: Whip cream until stiff. Fold cream into cooled chocolate mixture, then fold in egg whites.
Step 6: Line bottom and sides of 1½ quart straight-sided mold with Brownie Shell, cutting strips for sides and round for bottom of mold.

Step 7: Turn filling into cake-lined mold and cover with plastic wrap. Chill 3 to 4 hours, or until firm.

Step 8: Invert onto serving platter. Glaze with Chocolate Glaze. Let firm and decorate with chocolate curls. Cut into very thin slices to serve, as dessert is very rich.

BROWNIE SHELL

INGREDIENTS:

⅔ cup butter
4 squares unsweetened chocolate
2 cups sugar
4 eggs, well beaten
1½ cups flour
1 tsp. baking powder
½ tsp. salt
1 Tbsp. vanilla

PREPARATION:

Step 1: Melt butter with chocolate in saucepan over low heat. Remove from heat and add sugar and eggs.

Step 2: Combine flour, baking powder and salt and beat into chocolate mixture. Add vanilla.

Step 3: Line greased jellyroll pan with wax paper. Pour in batter, spread evenly. Bake at 350° 12 to 15 minutes or until cake springs back when lightly touched. Cake should be soft, not crisp.

Step 4: Turn out on rack and cool. Invert on clean towel and carefully peel off paper.

CHOCOLATE GLAZE:

Place 4 squares of semisweet chocolate and 3 Tbsps. strong coffee in top of double boiler and melt over hot water.

This is a "fussy" dessert, but not as difficult as it sounds. Make it the day before when you have time. This is what my mother called "company dessert". It will serve 20 people.

This cake is a snap to make, and for the devout chocoholic absolutely wonderful.

CHOCOLATE FUDGE CAKE

INGREDIENTS:

    1 (18½ ounce) package chocolate pudding
       cake mix
    1 cup sour cream
    4 large eggs
    1 cup oil
    1 (4-ounce) package instant chocolate
       fudge pudding
    ½ cup warm water
    ½ cup coffee-flavor liqueur
    1 (12 ounce) package semisweet
       chocolate pieces
    Powdered sugar
    ½ tsp. ground cinnamon
    Grated orange peel (coarsly grated, and enough
       to sprinkle over top of cake.)

PREPARATION:

Step 1: Combine in large bowl chocolate cake mix, sour cream, eggs, oil, chocolate pudding, warm water and cof-fee.flavored liqueur.

Step 2: Stir to blend then beat 3 mins. at medium speed. Stir in chocolate pieces.

Step 3: Turn into greased and floured 10 inch Bundt pan and bake at 350° 50 minutes or until cake tests done.

Step 4: Let cake sit in pan on rack for ten mins. or until you see it pulling from sides. Invert on another rack and let cool.

Step 5: Sprinkle with powdered sugar (put sugar in strainer and shake evenly over top of cake), add cinnamon and garnish with orange peel.

TURTLE CAKE

INGREDIENTS:

    1 (1 pound 2½ ounce) package German
       chocolate cake mix
    ½ cup butter or margarine, softened
    1½ cups water
    ½ cup oil
    1 (14 ounce) can sweetened condensed milk
    Chopped pecans
    1 (1 pound) package caramels
    Frosting

PREPRATION:

Step 1: Combine chocolate cake mix, butter, water, oil and ½ can of sweetened condensed imilk in mixing bowl. Mix well.

Step 2: Pour half of batter into greased and floured 13x9-inch baking dish.

Step 3: Bake at 350° 20 to 25 minutes.

Step 4: Melt and mix together caramels and remaining condensed milk over low heat until smooooth. Spread over baked cake layer. Sprinkle generously with chopped pecans.

Step 5: Cover with remaining cake batter, return to oven and bake 25 to 35 minutes longer or untilk cake tests done. Cool on rack and then spread with frosting.

FROSTING

INGREDIENTS:

½ cup butter or margarine
3 Tbsp. cocoa powder
6 Tbsps. evaporated milk
1 (1 pound) package powdered sugar, sifted
1 Tbsp. vanilla

PREPARATION:

Step 1: Combine butter, cocoa and evaporated milk in sauce pan. Melt over low heat

Step 2: Remove from heat and beat in powdered sugar and vanilla until smooth. Spread immediately.

Note: Since cake is very sweet, cut into very small pieces.

This is a great freezer dessert for company dinner. It might seem more difficult than it is, but your guests will think you are a "wonder" for making it. It also can be made the day before serving.

CHOCOLATE MOUSSE TORTE

INGREDIENTS:

¼ cup sifted cocoa powder
⅓ cup boiling water
¼ cup unsalted butter
½ tsp. vanilla

Dash salt
¾ cup sugar
1 egg
½ tsp baking soda
½ cup sour cream
1 cup sifted flour
¼ cup finely chopped walnut pieces
Mousse
Glaze

PREPARATION:

Step 1: Combine cocoa and boiling water in small bowl until smooth. Set aside

Step 2: Cream butter in large bowl of electric mixer. Add vanilla, salt and sugar. Beat until mixed well. Add egg, beating until smooth.

Step 3: Stir soda into sour cream in small bowl. Using low speed, add flour to egg mixture in 3 additions, alternating with sour cream and scraping bowl with rubber spatula and beating only until smooth after each addition

Step 4: Add cocoa and walnuts and beat only until smooth. Pour batter into well greased and floured 10-inch springform pan. Shake pan and rotate slightly to level top.

Step 5: Bake at 350° for 25 to 30 minutes, or until layer barely begins to shrink from sides of pan. Cool in pan 1 hour.

Step 6: Place Mousse over cooled cake in springform pan. Level top and place in freezer to set at least two hours.

Step 7: Remove cake from freezer. Run paring knife around sides of pan and remove sides. Place cake on rack with foil paper underneath to catch glaze.

Step 8: Pour thickened glaze over mousse layer, allowing it to run down sides. Use palette knife to spread and smooth. Glaze around sides.

MOUSSE

INGREDIENTS:

12 ounces semisweet chocolate
4 egg yolks
1 whole egg
1 tsp. instant coffee powder
1½ cups whipping cream
3 Tbsps. powdered sugar
4 egg whites

PREPARATION:

Step 1: Melt chocolate over simmering water. Combine yolks, whole egg and instant coffee powder. Whip until light and creamy, Blend in melted chocolate.

Step 2: Whip cream and sugar until fairly firm peaks form. Fold chocolate mixture into cream.

Step 3: Whip whites at high speed until moist and fluffy but not dry. Fold whites into chocolate mixture.

GLAZE
INGREDIENTS:

3 ounces semisweet chocolate
3 Tbsps. granulated sugar
2 Tbsps. water
2 Tbsps. unsalted butter at room temperature

PREPARATION:

Step 1: Break up chocolate and place in top of double boiler. Add sugar and water. Place over hot water on moderate heat. Stir occasionally until chocolate is melted and mixture is smooth.

Step 2: Remove from hot water. Add butter and stir until smooth. Let stand at room temperature, stirring occasionally, until mixture thickens slightly.

All right, already...enough with the chocolate (until later). Let's do a couple of simple recipes that your family will love.

This recipe was given to me by Vincent Price, but, in keeping with his evil movie persona, he left out one very important step in the cooking process. Fortunately I figured out how to beat the fiend at his devilish game.

PRICELESS BREAD PUDDING

INGREDIENTS:

1 cup firmly packed dark brown sugar
3 slices bread (I prefer egg bread, but it isn't the least neccessary)
2 Tbsps. softened butter
1 scant cup raisins or currants (the amount is optional — I prefer a little less)

                    3 eggs
                    2 cups milk
                    ⅛ tsp. salt
                    1½ Tbsps. white sugar
                    1 tsp. vanilla
PREPARATION:
Step 1: Loosely pack brown sugar in top of double boiler.
Step 2: Butter three slices of bread with softened butter, and then
         dice bread. Sprinkle over brown sugar. Add raisins or
         currants, scattering them over bread.
Step 3: Beat eggs, milk, salt, vanilla and white sugar together.
Step 4: Pour egg mixture over bread cubes but DO NOT
         STIR.
Step 5: Place over simmering water, cover (that's the part Vin-
         cent neglected to tell me) and cook 1 hour.
     Serve cold or at room temperature. Turn out onto serving
plate (preferably one with raised sides to catch the sauce). The
brown sugar has by this time developed into the most delicious
sauce.

     This recipe is for one of my absolute favorites. And why not? It
involves only thousands of calories; but just once in a while a little
wickedness isn't too dreadful. Really it's not! Really!

CREAM BRULEE
(Notice I avoided the word "CREME")

INGREDIENTS:
                    3 cups heavy (whipping) cream
                    6 Tbsps. granulated sugar
                    6 egg yolks (save the whites for a meringue)
                    2 tsps. vanilla
                    ½ cup brown sugar
PREPARATION:
Preheat oven to slow (300°)
Step 1: Heat cream over low heat and stir in granulated sugar
         until it is dissolved.
Step 2: Beat egg yolks until light, and pour hot cream over them
         gradually, stirring vigorously with wooden spoon. Do not
         use whisk.
Step 3: Stir in vanilla and salt and strain the mixture into
         individual baking dishes.

Step 4: Place baking dishes in baking pan containing 1 inch of hot water. Bake 50 to 60 minutes until silver knife inserted in center comes out clean. Do not overcook. Custard will continue to cook from retained heat.

Cool custard cups on rack and then chill thoroughly. Before serving, cover the surface of each cup with brown sugar, strained through a sieve. Set the dishes on bed of cracked ice and put under the broiler until sugar is brown and bubbly. Watch this process very carefully. It takes only a moment, and you don't want the sugar to burn.

Serve immediately (the texture of the warm crisp sugar and the cold custard is irresistible) or chill again and serve cold.

Now that so many delicious fruits are flash frozen (not in syrup) this recipe can be an all-season treat. Of course, the fresh fruits are better, but they are seasonal.

This dessert (with a nice bowl of soup first) makes a hearty supper.

WARM BERRY AND PEACH SHORTCAKE:

INGREDIENTS:
> 1½ cups blueberries
> 1 Tbsp. granulated sugar
> ½ tsp. lemon juice
> ¼ tsp cornstarch
> Dash salt
> 1 large peach, peeled and cut into eighths
> 1½ cups raspberries
> 1 Tbsp. raspberry liqueur (this is optional but preferable)
> ½ cup whipping cream
> 1 Tbsp. vanilla
> 2 Tbsps. powdered sugar
> 4 shortcake biscuits

PREPARATION:
Step 1: Combine blueberries, granulated sugar, lemon juice, cornstarch and salt in non-aluminum saucepan. Bring to boil, reduce heat and simmer over low heat until blueberrries break up and juice thickens, stirring occasionally to prevent sticking.
Step 2: Add peach slices and heat about 1 minute, then carefully fold in raspberries and raspberry liqueur. Mixture should be slightly warm.
Step 3: Beat cream until frothy. Beat in vanilla and powdered sugar until stiff but not dry.
Step 4: Split biscuits and place bottom halves in dessert bowls. Top each with ¼ berry mixture. Garnish with dollop of whipped cream. Place top half of biscuit slightly off center and serve at once.

SHORTCAKE BISCUITS
INGREDIENTS:

>2 cups unsifted white flour
>Sugar
>1 Tbsp. baking powder
>½ tsp. salt
>¼ cup unsalted butter, cut into ½
>   teaspoon-size bits and frozen
>Heavy (whipping) cream (1 cup plus 1 Tbsp.)
>1 egg yolk

PREPARATION:
Step 1: Mix together flour, 1½ Tbsps. sugar, baking powder and salt. Add frozen butter bits and blend quickly until butter is broken up into pieces the size of small peas. Add 1 cup whipping cream. Stir with fork to mix until just moistened.
Step 2: Turn out onto lightly floured board and knead 10 times. Small lumps of butter will be visible.
Step 3: Roll out to ¾ inch thickness, keeping dough square shaped.
Step 4: Cut into 8 (3 by 2 inch) rectangles. Place biscuits on ungreased baking sheet and brush with egg yolk mixed with 1 Tbsp. whipping cream. Sprinkle with 1½ Tbsps. sugar.
Step 5: Bake at 350° for 15 minutes or until golden brown.

I realize it is easier to make biscuits from packaged mix, but it can't compare to the "shortness" of these rich shortcakes. Incidentally, this recipe makes more than the amount needed, but the biscuits can be frozen and used later with some other fruit shortcake.

This recipe is simple and refreshing after a heavy dinner. You can use fresh or frozen strawberries (not the ones in sugar syrup).

ICED STRAWBERRY SOUFFLE

INGREDIENTS:

> 1½ pints strawberries
> 4 eggs (separated)
> ¾ cup sugar
> ½ cup whipping cream

PREPARATION:

Step 1: In a blender, puree strawberries with ½ cup sugar.

Step 2: Separate eggs; beat yolks with 1 cup of fruit puree; beat whites to form soft peaks, then beat in another ¼ cup sugar.

Step 3: In another bowl, whip ½ cup of cream.

Step 4: Gently stir some of whites into fruit and egg yolk mixture. Fold in rest of whites without overstirring. Now fold in whipped cream.

Step 5: Turn into 6 cup souffle dish and freeze.

Serve with remaining puree as a sauce.

Remove from freezer ten minutes before serving time to soften a bit.

Do you remember a few pages back when I left you with six egg whites left over from the Cream Brulee? Here is a dandy way to use them up.

MERINGUE RING

INGREDIENTS:

> 6 egg whites
> 1 cup granulated sugar
> 1 tsp. white vinegar
> 1 tsp. vanilla
> ⅛ tsp. cream of tartar
> Pinch of salt

PREPARATION:

Step 1: Beat egg whites until almost stiff. Add sugar slowly to whites, beating until meringue has a nice sheen.

Step 2: Carefully stir in vinegar, vanilla and cream of tartar until blended well.

Step 3: Lightly oil a ring mold and spoon in mix.

Step 4: Place mold in pan of warm water and bake at 300° for 40 minutes.

Meringue will be very pale. Let cool and then place in refrigerator to chill. Fill center with Rum Custard Sauce (after unmolding) and surround with fresh berries of your choice.

RUM CUSTARD SAUCE

INGREDIENTS:

> 2 egg yolks (Now I've stuck you with two more egg whites)*
> 1 cup powdered sugar
> 1 cup whipping cream
> Light rum (to taste)

PREPARATION:

Step 1: Beat yolks until pale yellow, and add powdered sugar slowly.

Step 2: Whip cream until fairly stiff, then fold into egg mixture, Add rum to taste.

*By the way, egg whites (not yolks) freeze beautifully. Put each egg white in a sandwich-size plastic bag and freeze. Let thaw at room temperature and they're good as new.

We all have tasted pineapple upside-down cake at sometime or other in our lives, but have you ever tried making one with fresh pineapple? Here is the recipe.

FRESH PINEAPPLE UPSIDE-DOWN CAKE

INGREDIENTS:

> ¼ cup unsalted butter
> ½ cup dark brown sugar, packed
> 2 Tbsps. dark rum
> 1 small, ripe pineapple, peeled, cored and
>   cut into at least 8 rings
> 12 pecan halves
> Cake layer

PREPARATION:

Step 1: Preheat oven to 350°. Combine butter, brown sugar and rum in 11-inch cast-iron skillet. Place skillet in heated oven and bake 7 to 10 minutes or until butter and sugar are melted. Mix well.

Step 2: Arrange pineapple rings in bottom of skillet as tightly as possible. Cut some in half, if necessary, to cover surface. Place pecan halves, rounded sides down, in center of rings. Set pan aside.

Step 3: Prepare Cake Layer batter and pour over pineapple in skillet. Smooth top of batter.

Step 4: Bake at 350° 40 to 45 minutes or until cake is deep golden brown and toothpick inserted in center comes out clean. Cool cake thoroughly on rack then turn out onto serving plate.

CAKE LAYER

INGREDIENTS:

> 2 cups sifted **cake flour**
> 2 tsps. baking powder
> ¼ tsp. salt
> ½ cup unsalted butter (softened)
> 1 cup sugar
> 2 eggs
> 2 tsps. vanilla
> 1 cup pineapple juice

PREPARATION:
Step 1: Sift flour, baking powder and salt together. Set aside.
Step 2: Cream butter and sugar in bowl of electric mixer until fluffy, about 3 minutes. Add dry mixture a little at a time, beating until well incorporated. (Mixture will be stiff at this point.)
Step 3: Add eggs, one at a time, beating well after each addition. Add vanilla and pineapple juice and beat well.

Every cook book in the world has recipes galore for pies of all sorts, but when you say "pie" to me I think only of **APPLE PIE.** To me there is no better breakfast than a slice of apple pie and a cup of coffee. And is there anything better than a piece of apple pie and a glass of milk before bedtime?

I don't like it mucked around with, either. I don't care for Dutch Apple pie, Bourbon Apple pie, or any of the variations on the plain old American apple pie. Leave well-enough alone, say I.

I do, however, have two pie recipes I occasionally serve. They are unusual enough to elicit a few "oohs and aahs", so I thought I might share them with you. They are simple to do since the advent of good frozen pie shells. (or the folded over pie crusts you find in the refrigerated sections of any good market.)

WILLAS' PECAN PIE

INGREDIENTS
1 basic 9-inch pie shell (uncooked)
8 ounces cream cheese
⅓ cup sugar and
¼ cup of sugar
4 eggs
2 tsps. vanilla
¼ tsp. salt
1¼ cup coarsely chopped pecans (I toast these in a moderate oven for 10 mins.)
1 cup dark corn syrup

PREPARATION:
Step 1: Beat cream cheese with ⅓ cup of sugar, 1 egg and 1 tsp. vanilla until light and creamy.
Step 2: Beat 3 eggs slightly. Add ¼ cup sugar, 1 tsp. vanilla and 1 cup corn syrup. Blend well.

Step 3: Spread cream cheese mixture in bottom of pastry shell. Sprinkle with toasted pecans. Top with corn syrup mix.

Step 4: Bake in 375° oven for 35 to 40 minutes or until center is firm. Cool on wire rack.

PAPAYA-MACADAMIA NUT PIE

INGREDIENTS:

> 1 baked 9.inch pie shell
> 6 ounces cream cheese
> 1½ Tbsps. sugar
> 1 tsp. grated orange peel
> 2 or 3 fresh papayas, sliced thinly
> 1 cup apricot preserves
> ½ cup finely chopped macadamia nuts
> ¼ cup orange juice
> 1 tsp. plain gelatin
> 1 cup whipping cream

PREPARATION:

Step 1: Whip cream cheese and orange peel until light and fluffy. Whip in sugar and spread over bottom of cooked (and cooled) pie crust.

Step 2: Arrange papaya slices in overlapping pattern on top of cream cheese so that fruit makes a pretty design.

Step 3: Soften the gelatin in the orange juice.

Step 4: Heat the apricot jam until melted, push through a strainer and then return to saucepan and reheat. Add orange juice mixture and stir until gelatin has melted. Cool and then pour glaze over top of the papaya.

Step 5: Sprinkle macadamia nuts to make 1-inch band around the outer edge of pie. Put in refrigerator and chill.

Step 6: Whip cream with a little sugar and vanilla. Place small dollop in center of pie, and serve extra whipped cream, to be added if wanted.

There is no denying the fact that the best chocolate chip cookie recipe in the world belongs to a certain Mrs. Fields. I've tried to analyze the ingredients but the closest I can get to them is the following recipe. I think these cookies are almost as good...but not quite. That explains why she's rich, and I'm not.

Give my recipe a try, anyway, and remember to serve them warm from the oven as Mrs. Fields does. (That's why they are soft.)

SOFT CHOCOLATE CHIP COOKIES

INGREDIENTS:

1 cup bttter (softened)
1 cup granulated sugar
1 cup light brown sugar
2 eggs
1 tsp. vanilla
2 cups flour
2½ cups oats (such as Quaker oats)
½ tsp. salt
1 tsp. baking powder
1 tsp. baking soda
1 (12-ounce) package semisweet
chocolate pieces.
1 (4-ounce) bar of milk chocolate, grated.
(If you can find a good European imported chocolate, it's worth the added expense.)
1½ cup chopped macadamia nuts.

PREPARATION:

Step 1: Cream together butter and sugars. Add eggs and vanilla, beating well.

Step 2: Mix together flour, oats, salt, baking powder and baking soda. Place small amounts in blender and process until mixture turns into powder.

Step 3: Mix butter-egg mixture with flour mixture until just blended. Add chocolate pieces, milk chocolate and chopped nuts.

Step 4: Roll into balls about size of golf ball and place 2 inches apart on ungreased baking sheet. Bake in 375° oven for 12 minutes.

Makes about 3 dozen cookies.

You can make the batter up ahead of time and keep in cool place. Remember, you want to serve the cookies warm (not hot).

PEANUT BUTTER COOKIES
TO MAKE YOU GO WILD

INGREDIENTS:

>1 cup butter (softened)
>1 cup creamy peanut butter
>1 cup granulated sugar
>1 cup brown sugar (dark)
>2 eggs
>2 cups flour
>1 tsp. baking soda
>1 (6-ounce) package semisweeet chocolate pieces
>½ cup chopped roasted peanuts

PREPARATION:

Step 1: Cream butter and peanut butter, Gradually add sugars until blended. Add eggs, one at a time.

Step 2: Sift flour, measure and sift again. Add soda to flour and stir it all into creamed mixture. Stir in chocolate and peanuts.

Step 3: Drop by tsps.onto greased baking sheet and flatten slightly with back of spoon.

Step 4: Bake in 350° oven for 15 to 20 minutes. Makes about 6 dozen cookies.

I hope you have found some recipes to give you pleasure in these few pages. Have fun cooking them....that's what it's all about!

ABOUT THE AUTHOR

Robert Quarry was born and raised in Santa Rosa, Calif., where, he says, his early culinary influences were a marvelous mixture of Italian, French, Spanish and Chinese cooking; influences that led to his avocation as a chef.

His vocation, however, is as an actor, a career of some forty years. He began his career in radio during World War II, appearing on many of the top shows of the time, including Lux Radio Theater where he was a member of that famed show's stock company.

After serving in the Army for two years he moved to New York and began a successful career during the early days of television, appearing on such memorable shows as Studio One, Philco Playhouse, Kraft Theater, Hallmark Hall Of Fame and Playhouse 90.

He made his Broadway debut co-starrring with Katharine Hepburn in "As You Like It", and after several successful plays was brought to Hollywood to appear with Joanne Woodward in "A Kiss Before Dying".

He has guest-starred on most of the top-rated dramatic series on television, but is probably best remembered for a series of horror films made while under contract to American International Pictures, most notably the "Count Yorga, Vampire" films and "Dr. Phibes Rises Again", co-starring with Vincent Price.

His cookbook, "You Can't Barbecue a Taco", will be published in the fall of '89.

NOTES

NOTES

NOTES

NOTES

NOTES